TAMING THE MIND

Also by Thubten Chodron:

Buddhism for Beginners (Snow Lion Publications)

Working with Anger (Snow Lion Publications)

Open Heart, Clear Mind (Snow Lion Publications)

Arya Tara: A Star by Which to Navigate (Snow Lion Publications)

Interfaith Insights (Timeless Books)

Blossoms of the Dharma: Living as a Buddhist Nun (North Atlantic Books)

Transforming the Heart: The Buddhist Way to Joy and Courage (by Geshe Jampa Tegchok, edited by Thubten Chodron) (Snow Lion Publications)

Choosing Simplicity (by Venerable Bhikshuni Master Wu Yin, edited by Thubten Chodron) (Snow Lion Publications)

TAMING
the MIND

Bhikshuni
THUBTEN CHODRON

SNOW LION PUBLICATIONS
Ithaca, New York ✦ Boulder, Colorado

Snow Lion Publications
P.O. Box 6483
Ithaca, New York 14851 USA
(607) 273-8519
www.snowlionpub.com

Printed in Canada on acid-free recycled paper.

ISBN 1-55939-221-5

Library of Congress Cataloging-in-Publication Data

Thubten Chodron, 1950-
    Taming the mind / Thubten Chodron.
        p.   cm.
    Includes bibliographical references.
    ISBN 1-55939-221-5 (alk. paper)
    1. Religious life—Buddhism. 2. Buddhism—Doctrines.
I. Title.
BQ5395.T488   2004
294.3'444—dc22

                                              2004011912

Text typeset in Adobe Garamond
by Richard E. Farkas

CONTENTS

FOREWORD

I am very happy to know that Ven. Thubten Chodron has prepared another book, *Taming the Mind*. In the course of living in both the West and Asia, where she has studied and taught Buddhism, she has acquired a keen appreciation of the various Buddhist traditions as well as of the misunderstandings that sometimes arise about them.

This book helps to overcome such misconceptions, showing how to find peace and contentment through a practical application of the teachings of the compassionate Buddha. Ven. Thubten Chodron has chosen a wide variety of situations that we encounter in daily life and has explained how to deal with them from a Buddhist viewpoint, in words that are easy to understand. In doing so, she has made a valuable contribution to peace and human understanding by providing her readers with the opportunity not only to understand a variety of approaches to Buddhist practice, but also to benefit from such practices in their own lives.

March 3, 2004

INTRODUCTION

A student approached me after a talk at the National University of Singapore. "One of my friends isn't a Buddhist, but she wants to learn about it. Is there an introductory book in simple English that's easy to understand and that explains the essence of Buddha's teachings?"

I knew that question well. In fact, I had searched for such a book but to no avail. There is a variety of excellent material on Buddhism, but none of it fits the above description.

This started me thinking. Several weeks later, a student from the polytechnic queried, "Is there a book about friendship, love, and marriage from a Buddhist viewpoint? Something we twenty-first century young people can relate to?"

Again, I drew a blank. The idea of writing *Taming the Mind* was born soon thereafter.

Overview

Taming the Mind is for anyone interested in Buddha's teachings. The first section, "An Outlook on the World and a Way of Life," contains the essence of Buddhist philosophy and psychology together with practical ways they can be put to use in daily life. The second section discusses how to have good relationships with others. The third section, "Taming Bad Habits, Cultivating Good Ones," gives pointers for how to practice the Dharma in our daily life interactions. The fourth section, "The Spread of the Buddha's Teachings," relates the history and development of Buddhism and explains the meaning of Buddhist temples, centers, ceremonies, and festivals. "Buddhism Today" remedies two potential harms: superstitions and misconceptions about Buddhism and religious intolerance in our world.

Each section of the book can be read on its own. Thus, if you are more interested in "Our Relationships with Others," read that section first, and later go back to the first section. At the end of the book are a glossary and a list for additional reading for your use.

Through taming our minds, we can contact our inner beauty and human potential. This book gives an inkling how this can be done.

Language

I've attempted to avoid complicated technical terms as much as possible and to express the Buddha's teachings in clear and simple English. Nevertheless, using some technical terms is unavoidable. Translating these terms into English isn't always easy and the resulting words sometimes sound strange to the ear. However, with time, these words will sound less awkward. Their meaning is given in the text and a glossary is provided at the end of the book.

Using he/she or s/he to express the impersonal third-person pronoun is awkward. Thus, "he" and "she" are used alternately. However, the reference isn't restricted to a person of a particular gender.

Acknowledgments

My gratitude and respect go first to my teachers, principally His Holiness the Dalai Lama, Tsenzhap Serkong Rinpoche, and Zopa Rinpoche. Without the kindness and support—both material and moral—of people too numerous to mention, this book couldn't have been written. Still, a few names must be mentioned. The students of the Buddhist societies of Singapore's five tertiary institutes inspired the writing of this book. The members of Dharma Friendship Foundation in Seattle, USA, provided the circumstances and encouraged me to write. Heartfelt thanks also go to Steve Wilhelm and Cindy Loth for editing the manuscript and to Lesley Lockwood, Pua Yeow Khoon, Loh Hung Leong, Yeo Soo Hwa, and Shira Lee for their valuable suggestions. I also thank Ven. Dhammika, Ven. Jendy, and Ven. Sangye Khadro for checking the chapters on Theravada, Mahayana, and Tibetan Buddhism respectively. All errors are my own.

Bhikshuni Thubten Chodron
Vesak (The Buddha's Enlightenment Day)
June 3, 2004

I   AN OUTLOOK ON THE WORLD
AND A WAY OF LIFE

We may wonder, "How did I get here? Why was I born? Who am I, and why do certain things happen to me and not to others? How does my mind influence my experience?"

To find the answers, we start to look beyond this present life to our situation in general, and we seek solutions to unsatisfactory conditions on a wider scale. What is our potential as human beings? Who can guide us to actualize it, and what direction do we take to do so? As our view broadens and deepens, so does our ability to make our lives meaningful through developing compassion and wisdom.

1   MIND IS THE CREATOR OF OUR EXPERIENCE

Mind is the forerunner of all actions,
All deeds are led by mind, created by mind.
If one speaks or acts with a corrupt mind,
Suffering follows, as wheels follow the hoof of a draught-ox.

Mind is the forerunner of all actions,
All deeds are led by mind, created by mind.
If one speaks or acts with a serene mind,
Happiness follows, as surely as one's shadow.

The Dhammapada

According to Buddhism, mind is the creator or source of our experience. This has profound significance: Because we each have a mind over which we have some degree of control, we are ultimately responsible for our own experiences. It's unrealistic to blame others for our problems if our own energy is the source of these problems. Similarly, to experience happiness, we needn't placate an external being but must create the cause for happiness within ourselves by developing positive states of mind.

The Buddhist meaning of "mind" refers to the entire spectrum of perceptions, emotions, and cognitions that we have. It includes what we call "heart" in English (as in, "He has a good heart.") The mind isn't just the intellect nor is it the physical organ of the brain. Formless, the mind isn't made of atoms, so it can't be seen or measured with scientific instruments.

Mind is what experiences pleasure and pain, what thinks, sees, hears, smells, tastes, and touches. The mind is clarity and awareness, for it reflects objects of perception and becomes involved with them. Although the term "our mind" may be used, it doesn't refer to a universal shared mind, but to each of our individual minds. "Mindstream" refers to the continuity of mind from moment to moment.

There are two principal ways our minds create our experiences. First, the mind motivates our actions, or karma. The imprints of our actions are stored on our mindstreams. When these karmic imprints mature, they influence the situations we encounter. Secondly, our minds interpret and discriminate whatever we contact, thus filtering our perceptions. By doing this, our minds determine how we experience the events in our lives. Let's examine these two points in greater depth.

Mind as the Creator of Karma

In the *Rice Seedling Sutra,* the Buddha explained that our confused lives in cyclic existence are the results of our actions and that these actions originate from our minds. How does this occur? Ignorance, which is a wrong conception of the nature of reality, produces other afflictions—disturbing attitudes and negative emotions—such as anger, clinging attachment, jealousy, arrogance, and confusion. Motivated by afflictions, we act. These actions, or karma, leave imprints on the continuity of our minds (mindstreams). The karmic imprints, or potentials, are like residual energy remaining after we've finished an action. Intangible, they are carried along by our mindstreams. When the environment is conducive, certain karmic potentials mature and influence what we experience.

This process is complex and generally takes time to understand fully. What follows is a brief description to give you a general idea.

From a Buddhist perspective, our minds are presently obscured by ignorance: We don't understand who we are in the deepest sense or the way in which people and phenomena exist. Unaware of our ultimate nature, we misconceive ourselves to be solid and real and to be an independent self. This misconception of the self is apparent when we experience a strong emotion. For example, when we're angry, we feel there's a real "I" who is justifiably irate. But if we ask ourselves, "Who is angry?" we have a hard time pointing to exactly who or what this seemingly independent self is. In fact, our self or "I" exists but not in the way we think it does.

We seek to protect and please this independent self, which is a creation of our misconceptions. Thus, we become attached to whatever gives us pleasure and have aversion toward the people and things that interfere with our happiness. From this ignorant view of ourselves spring jealousy, pride, confusion, grudge-holding, laziness, and an assortment of other undesirable personality characteristics. These afflictions obscure our good qualities, preventing us from being the kind of people we would like to be.

Motivated by these afflictions, we act. "Karma" refers to the intentional actions of our body, speech, and mind: what we think, say, and do. Our actions stem from our minds. First, a motivation arises in our minds, then we act. Sometimes, we're unaware of our motivations and are surprised at what we do and say. But if we're attentive, we'll observe that all our actions are preceded by motivations.

For example, before we criticize someone, the thought arises, "This person is making me unhappy. I want him to stop." Then we speak angrily, telling another his defects. The Buddha explained that this action leaves an imprint on our mindstream, and later, when the external situation in our lives is conducive, this karmic potential matures and determines our experience.

Just as a small seed can grow into a tree with many fruits, this one action of criticizing someone can produce several results: Others will criticize us, our environment will be inhospitable, we'll habitually criticize others, and we'll have an unfortunate rebirth.

Similarly, when we have good motivations, ones that are unselfish and concerned with others' benefit, we act constructively. Such actions leave positive imprints on our consciousness. These positive imprints likewise give rise to results: Others will like us, our habitat will be pleasant, and we'll have good personalities and a fortunate rebirth.

Thus, at different times, we generate afflictions such an anger, attachment, and confusion, and positive emotions and attitudes such as love, self-respect, consideration for others, and wisdom. The Buddhist path is one of eliminating afflictions and increasing positive mental states, in order to bring ourselves and those around us peace and happiness.

Taking Rebirth

Through his deep insight into how things exist, the Buddha observed that due to afflictions and karma, our minds continue to take one rebirth after another. At the time of death, we ordinary beings mentally cling to our bodies and to our lives. We're afraid to separate from our bodies and to leave everything around us. When it becomes obvious that we're departing from this body and life, we grasp for another body.

These two—craving and grasping—act as the cooperative conditions for karmic imprints to ripen at the time of death. As these karmic imprints start to mature, our minds are attracted to other bodies, and we seek to take rebirth in them. In the case of a human rebirth, after passing through an intermediate state between one life and the next, our consciousness then enters a fertilized egg. We develop the aggregates of a human being—a human body and mind.

In this new rebirth, we perceive people and things through our senses. Experiencing pleasant or unpleasant feelings due to these sense perceptions, we generate attachment, hostility, or indifference. These emotions cause us to act. Our actions leave more imprints on our mindstreams, and at the time of death, we're again propelled to take rebirth in another body.

This cycle of rebirth is called *samsara*. Samsara isn't a place: it isn't our world. Rather, samsara—also called cyclic existence—is our situation of taking one rebirth after another under the control of afflictions and karmic actions.

Thus, our own energy causes us to be reborn as who we are, in our present circumstance. However, karma isn't "cast in concrete," and our lives aren't predetermined. Which karmic imprints ripen depends on our environment and our state of mind. In addition, we have the ability to control our actions and, thus, to shape our future.

The law of karma is the functioning of cause and effect within our mindstreams. Whether we experience pain or pleasure depends on what we have done in the past. Our previous actions or karma were motivated by our minds. In this way, our minds are the principal creator of our experience.

Was There a Beginning?

Some people wonder, "How did this process start? Was there a beginning to our universe and the beings in it?"

The physical evolution of our universe is a matter for scientific research. Science examines the continuity of physical material in our universe—how cause and effect operate physically to produce the various things in our universe.

The matter in our universe has a cause: a previous moment of matter or energy (as shown in Einstein's equation, $E=mc^2$). It would be difficult to prove there was a time when neither matter nor energy existed. If there once was nothing, then out of what did matter arise? How could things be produced without causes? Our present universe is a transformation of physical energy that existed previously.

A mind isn't made of physical material, and therefore its causes aren't material. A mind arises from the previous moment of mind in its continuity. We can trace our consciousness back moment by moment to childhood. Our mind has changed since then, but our present mind is related to and caused by our mind when we were younger.

In this way, the existence of our mindstream can be traced back to the time of conception. The consciousness that entered the fertilized egg in our mother's womb must also have had a cause. From a Buddhist perspective, this is a previous moment of mind, i.e., our consciousness of a previous life. This continuity of mind goes back infinitely. There was no beginning. Just as the mathematical number line has no beginning—one more can always be added—neither does the continuity of our consciousness.

Our afflictions, which include ignorance, also arise from causes: the previous moments of afflictions. Their continuity goes back infinitely. If there were a first moment of afflictions, then we would be able to point to what caused it. If we were initially pure and later became ignorant, where did ignorance come from? It's impossible for pure beings who perceive reality to later become ignorant. If someone becomes ignorant, he or she wasn't completely pure before.

Nor can another being make us ignorant. No one can put ignorance into our mindstreams the way water is put into a cup.

From a Buddhist point of view, it's senseless to search for the beginning of our existence and the start of our afflictions. The Buddha was extremely practical, stressing that we deal with the present situation and try to remedy it. Getting lost in useless speculation prevents us from focusing on the present and improving it.

For example, a person is hit by a car and lies bleeding in the street. Before he'll accept medical attention, he insists on knowing who was driving the car, who manufactured it, and when it was made. While seeking this information, he dies. We would say such a person is foolish. Knowing the origin of the car doesn't change his injury. Nor does it save his life. He would have been wiser to deal with his present situation, get medical attention, and recover.

Similarly, it's better to examine our present difficulties and their cause—

the afflictions—and remedy them, rather than to get lost in speculation about a non-existent beginning. The Buddha didn't discuss the origin of the universe because knowing that doesn't help us solve our problems or improve the quality of our lives. Instead, he explained how our minds cause our experience through motivating us to act. These actions leave karmic imprints on our mindstreams, which influence our future experiences. Understanding this enables us to gain control over and purify this process.

Mind as the Interpreter of Our Environment

The second way in which our minds create our experience is by interpreting the objects we perceive. How we interpret something determines how we experience it. Although we generally assume we accurately perceive what is "out there," our experiences are in fact colored by our interpretations and projections.

For example, when two people meet Joe, one likes him while the other doesn't. One sees Joe as considerate and intelligent, someone with a good sense of humor. The other perceives Joe as a person who makes fun of others and is competitive and insensitive to their feelings. Both assume they perceive Joe as he is. However, if that were true, they would perceive him the same way, and they clearly don't.

Both people hear the same words and voice when Joe speaks, yet they interpret what is said differently. Their minds move very quickly from perception—the sounds and sights they perceive through their senses—to conclusion—the meaning placed on the sense data.

Thus, one person experiences Joe's jokes as humorous and good-natured and thinks, "Joe is a nice person. I enjoy being with him." Thereafter, whenever he meets Joe, he sees a friend and expects to have a good time. The other interprets Joe's words as sarcastic and thinks, "Joe is egotistical. I don't like him." Later, when she meets him, she sees a disagreeable person and feels aversion.

Both people assume their perception of Joe is correct. But in fact, both relate to Joe through the veils of their own preconceptions. Joe's qualities of being friendly or obnoxious are created by the projections of the people perceiving him. In and of himself, Joe is neither.

How we look at a situation determines our experience of it. We may look at our mother and think, "She always tells me what to do. She's so demanding." Then every time we see her, we feel uncomfortable.

On the other hand, we may think, "My mother gave me this body. She took care of me when I was a helpless infant and couldn't even feed myself. She taught me how to speak and behave." Then our mother appears very kind to us. When we see her, she seems loving and we have affection for her.

Because we interpret certain behavior in others as harmful, we give them the label "enemies." Thereafter, they appear to us as enemies. Similarly, because we label other persons' behavior as kind and call them friends, that's how they appear to us. Friends and enemies actually come from our own minds. We create them. Having created our friends and enemies through the power of our minds, we then cling to our friends and try to harm our enemies. In fact, we're attached to or have aversion to what our own minds have created.

How we interpret our environment and the people in it depends on the purity of our minds. Just as the image reflected in a dirty mirror is unattractive and obscured, so too is the appearance of an object to a mind sullied by afflictions and negative karmic imprints. The same object reflected in a spotless mirror is clear and beautiful. Likewise, whatever is perceived by a pure mind is lovely.

Some mentally ill people believe the people around them are plotting to harm them. Overwhelmed by their fear, they may even see ghosts where there are none. Although they are convinced their perceptions are correct, we experience the same environment in a completely different way. This is due to the different actions we've done in the past as well as to the present functioning of our afflictions.

For a person advanced on the path to enlightenment, this earth is a pure land. For people whose minds are filled with anger, it's a fearful, hellish realm. The environment doesn't exist as pleasurable or painful in and of itself. Our experience of it depends on our previously created actions and our present interpretations. Both the hellish realms and the pure lands are created by our minds. Our minds are the source, the creator, of our experience.

Knowing this, we become aware that the only way to arrive at a state of lasting and perfect happiness is to purify our minds of their disturbing thoughts and the imprints and stains of our karma. We're responsible; we can do this. A modern Buddhist hymn based on a verse from the *Dhammapada* says:

By ourselves is evil done,
By ourselves we pain endure.
By ourselves we cease from wrong,
By ourselves become we pure.
No one saves us but ourselves;
No one can and no one may.
We ourselves must walk the path,
Buddhas merely show the way.

The Buddhas show us the path to follow. They know it because they have experienced it themselves. Those beings who are now Buddhas were once entrenched in their confusion and difficulties as we now are. However, by following the path, they purified their minds and developed their good qualities to the utmost, thereby becoming fully enlightened Buddhas. We have the potential to do the same.

The Buddhas guide us, but we must do the work. Just as our teachers can instruct us in grammar but can't learn it for us, so too can the Buddhas give us teachings and guidance, but we must put them into practice. In the *White Lotus of the Holy Dharma Sutra*, it says:

The Buddhas cannot wash away beings' negativities with water,
They cannot take beings' suffering out with their hands,
Nor can they transplant their realizations into others.
The Buddhas liberate beings by teaching them the truth of thusness
    (emptiness).

While Buddhism emphasizes self-responsibility, that doesn't mean we are alone on the path. We can rely on the guidance, blessings, and example of the Three Jewels: the Buddhas, Dharma, and Sangha.

The Buddhas are those beings who have purified all anger, attachment, ignorance, and selfishness from their minds. In addition, they have developed all good qualities such as impartial love, compassion, and wisdom.

The Dharma is the realizations of reality and the cessation of all problems and sufferings that our ignorance brings. In a general sense, the Dharma also refers to the Buddha's teachings, which lead us to gain realizations.

Sangha refers to anyone who has realized reality, or selflessness, the absence of an independently existing self. These people, who are well along the path to liberation and enlightenment, may be ordained (monks or nuns) or lay people. In a more general sense, the Sangha is the community of monks and nuns who have dedicated their lives to improving themselves and benefiting others.

In the upcoming chapters, we'll examine in greater depth how our minds create our experience. We'll also see how to tame the monkey mind—that unmanageable part of ourselves—so we can create the causes for happiness, make our lives meaningful, and have harmonious relationships with others.

2 THE FOUR NOBLE TRUTHS: CREATIVELY DEALING WITH DIFFICULTIES

The essence of the Buddha's teachings is expressed in the four noble truths. The first two truths are an accurate description of our present situation, and the last two show a practical way to improve it. We can validate the four noble truths through our own experience: a mystical leap of faith is not necessary to accept them.

These four facts are called noble because they are taught by the noble ones: those beings who have direct perception of reality. Also, by understanding these four, we too will be ennobled. They are truths because they are correct: It's true that sufferings and their causes are to be abandoned, and it's true that the cessation of sufferings and their causes and the path to attain this are to be adopted. These facts don't deceive us or lead us away from happiness. By understanding them, we'll enter the path to liberation and enlightenment.

The four noble truths are:

1. True sufferings
2. True causes of suffering
3. True cessation of sufferings and their causes
4. True path to that cessation

Sufferings are to be identified; their causes are to be abandoned; cessations of sufferings and their causes are to be realized; and the paths are to be practiced.

The First Truth: Suffering Exists

The Pali and Sanskrit word *dukkha* is often translated as "suffering." However, this English word is misleading because it connotes an extreme pain. Thus, some people falsely say, "My life is okay, I have no great problems. Why does Buddhism insist that life is suffering when in fact I experience much pleasure? Buddhism seems pessimistic!"

When the Buddha described our lives as dukkha, he was referring to any and all unsatisfactory conditions. These range from minor disappointments, problems, and difficulties to intense pain and misery. Therefore, throughout this book all these words will be used to indicate dukkha: the fact that things aren't completely right in our lives and could be better.

Although initially we may not like to think about unsatisfactory conditions in our lives, it's necessary to do so in order to remedy them. If someone is sick but refuses to acknowledge it, she won't seek medicine and thus won't recover. Similarly, if we pretend everything in our lives is fine, we won't look deeply to find the source of uneasiness and fear inside us. Without examining our own emotions and attitudes, we won't be able to subdue the disturbing ones and increase the positive ones. And without transforming our mind in this way, we won't be able to eliminate the causes of suffering, create the causes of happiness, and reach a state of lasting happiness. However, if we examine our situation clearly and acknowledge it, we'll be able to improve it. In addition, being honest with ourselves brings a sense of relief and hope, for we know our problems aren't insurmountable.

The Buddha described three types of dukkha, or unsatisfactory conditions, that we face:

1. The dukkha of pain
2. The dukkha of change
3. Pervasive compounded dukkha

The dukkha of pain occurs whenever we're mentally or physically miserable. Physical suffering includes headaches and scraped knees as well as the torment of cancer and heart attacks. Mental suffering occurs when we fail to get what we want, when we lose something we're attached to, or when misfortune comes our way. We're sad when our career goals don't succeed, we're depressed when we part from loved ones, we're anxious when the stock market goes down.

Mental and physical difficulties come to every living being, no matter where he or she lives. Technological progress may have eliminated many of our physical problems, but it also has created new ones—pollution and the threat of nuclear war. We may have a higher living standard than ever before, but we also have more crime, increased drug abuse, and a rise in suicide and divorce. Technology alone hasn't solved all our problems.

The dukkha of change indicates that activities we generally regard as pleasurable in fact inevitably change and become painful. Consider food, for example. We regard eating delicious food as a source of pleasure. If this were true, then the more we ate, the happier we would be. This obviously isn't the case. While eating initially eliminates the pain of hunger, continuous eating brings indigestion.

Similarly, we regard our friends as a source of pleasure. However, if pleasure intrinsically existed in being with our friends, then the more we were with them, the happier we would be. When we first see our friends, we're delighted and the pain of loneliness vanishes. But if they stay too long, we get tired and wish they would leave.

Although the objects and people around us give us some pleasure, too much of them makes us uncomfortable. The happiness we initially derive from them turns into unhappiness. This indicates that happiness was never in those activities, objects, or people but was a product of the interaction between us and them.

Pervasive compounded dukkha refers to our situation of having bodies and minds prone to pain. We can become miserable simply by the changing of external conditions. The weather changes and our bodies suffer from the cold; how a friend treats us changes and we become depressed.

This is called pervasive dukkha because our present bodies and minds are pervaded with the potential to experience pain. We have no foolproof way to protect ourselves from it. It's also called pervasive suffering because this unsatisfactory state afflicts all beings who haven't realized the reality of how people and phenomena exist. Even those people who seem to have all the pleasures life could offer still become old and die.

Our present bodies and minds compound our misery in the sense that they're the basis for our present problems. Our present bodies are the basis upon which we experience bad health. If we didn't have a body that was receptive to pain, we wouldn't fall ill no matter how many viruses and germs we were exposed to. Similarly, our present minds are the basis upon which we experience the pain of hurt feelings. If we had minds that weren't contaminated by anger, we wouldn't suffer from the mental anguish of conflict with others.

By being attached to our present bodies and minds, we act in ways that bring us more pain and confusion in the future. For example, to pamper our bodies, we may take others' possessions or lie to get what we want. Not only does this harm others, but it also leaves imprints in our own mindstreams that cause us to be deprived of possessions in the future.

Some people may feel forlorn after considering these three types of dukkha, for it seems we're in a terrible situation. They may think Buddhism is unduly pessimistic for talking so much about suffering. However, if we understand the purpose of the Buddha's teachings, such misconceptions won't arise, and instead we'll feel inspired.

The reason for thinking about the unsatisfactory state we're in is to generate within ourselves the determination to be free from it and to have lasting happiness in its place. With this earnest intention to improve our lives, we'll investigate the causes of our problems and apply methods to eliminate them. This gives our lives profound meaning and clear direction.

The Second Truth: Suffering Has Causes

As explained in the previous chapter, our minds are the source of our happiness and suffering. When we have wisdom and compassion, happiness follows; when we're confused by our afflictions, difficulties come. Therefore, it's important to differentiate between constructive and destructive states of mind so that we can increase the former and diminish the latter.

The chief cause of our problems is ignorance. Ignorance is a mental factor, or attitude, that obscures our understanding of who we are and the mode in which all phenomena exist. Not only does ignorance keep us from realizing how things exist, it also grasps things as existing in a way they do not.

For example, functioning things—things produced by causes and conditions, like a mountain, a pen, and our bodies—constantly change moment by moment. Under the influence of ignorance, however, we treat them as if they were unchanging and static. Thus, when we meet a friend we haven't seen for a long time, we're startled by how much she has aged. Similarly, we're surprised when things break, for although we may intellectually know they change, in our hearts we believe they are static. Although scientists tell us subatomic substances are in constant motion, when we look at a table, it appears solid and unchanging to us. Ignorance makes our perceptions not accord with reality.

A deeper level of ignorance is what Buddhists call the misconception of inherent existence. Many books have been written on this subject, and it takes time to identify our ignorance and how it functions. The misconception of inherent existence is the root of all our afflictions and problems. Thus, its remedy, the wisdom realizing emptiness (the wisdom realizing reality), is the heart of Buddhist teachings.

Inherent existence means that people and phenomena appear to us as if they exist in and of themselves, with an essential nature making them what they are. For example, a flower is composed of many parts—a stem, petals, stamen, and pistils. However, the flower appears to us as a single phenomenon with something in it that makes it inherently a flower.

Similarly, each person is composed of a body and a mind and on that basis is given his or her name. However, when we look at someone, there appears to be a real person there, someone who exists independently of his or her body and mind, independently of his or her name. This is what is meant by "inherent existence." Things falsely appear to be inherently existent, and we ignorantly assent to this appearance and grasp or conceive things to exist independently. Whereas everything exists dependently, we innately conceive everything to be independent.

This ignorance of the ultimate nature—that everything is empty of independent or inherent existence—is the root from which our other afflictions grow. It impacts our daily lives by making us attached to whatever seems pleasurable and averse, or even hostile, to whatever is displeasing. Under the influence of attachment and aversion, our moods roller-coaster from high to low each day.

Attachment overestimates the good qualities of a person or thing and then clings to that person, thing, place, or idea. Anger exaggerates the negative qualities of a person or thing and makes us want to harm it or get away from it. Disturbed by attachment and anger, most people—and animals too—spend their lives helping their friends and harming their enemies. Besides these three principal poisons—ignorance, attachment, and anger— other disturbing mental states influence us as well: jealousy, pride, laziness, grudge-holding, and so on.

In daily life, these afflictions influence our actions. For example, attachment to our own personal success may make us compete, rather than cooperate, with our colleagues at work. Anger impels us to lose our temper and insult others. We need only reflect on our actions, read the newspaper, or turn on the TV to see what attachment and anger cause people to do.

These actions, or karma, leave imprints on our mindstreams. As explained before, the imprints propel us to take rebirth and to experience unsatisfactory conditions wherever we're born.

Even positive actions, such as helping someone out of love, will bring only short-term happiness in the future as long as we're still influenced by ignorance. Lasting happiness comes only when all ignorance is removed. Thus, these two factors—afflictions and karma—are the causes of our constantly recurring problems.

The Third Truth: Suffering Can Be Eliminated

Afflictions and karma can be eliminated. They aren't the intrinsic nature of our minds. Since the afflictions arise from the misconception of ignorance, once we realize emptiness, or the nature of things as they are, ignorance no longer influences us. It's like turning on a light in a dark room: the darkness vanishes.

Through wisdom, we can cleanse ignorance and other afflictions from our mindstreams forever. Thus, we'll stop doing actions that propel us to take rebirth. In addition, wisdom cleanses the karmic imprints currently on our mindstreams, so they won't bring results.

A cessation is the lack of, or the stopping of, a certain affliction. A cessation is a negative phenomenon, i.e., it's an absence of an affliction. As we progress along the path and gradually eliminate the afflictions, the gross levels and then the subtle levels of anger, attachment, and ignorance will cease. When we've eliminated all afflictions from their roots, we'll attain nirvana or liberation, the cessation of all sufferings and all causes of suffering. In the *Dhammapada*, the Buddha said:

> Just as a rowboat is lightened
> When you bail all the water out,
> So too nirvana is attained
> When hate and greed are given up.

Nirvana is a blissful state, in which we'll no longer take rebirth under the influence of afflictions and karma. After death, people who have attained liberation single-pointedly meditate on reality—the emptiness of inherent existence—and thus abide in peace, with unceasing happiness.

People seeking self-liberation from cyclic existence are called either hearers or solitary realizers. The hearers are so called because they hear and then teach the Buddha's doctrine. The solitary realizers, in their last lifetime, attain nirvana in solitude, at a time when a Buddha isn't present. Hearers and solitary realizers who attain nirvana are called arhats, or foe destroyers, because they have destroyed the foe of afflictions.

Some people prefer to follow the bodhisattva path, aiming to become Buddhas in order to benefit all others. Even after they have ceased all their own afflictions and karma, bodhisattvas deliberately take rebirth in cyclic existence to guide and teach others. Their rebirths are motivated by compassion, not ignorance. Thus, they remain in the world to work for others.

While acting for the benefit of others, bodhisattvas work to eliminate the subtle stains on their own mindstreams so they can become fully enlightened Buddhas. Although bodhisattvas have such strong love and compassion for others that they vow not to attain enlightenment until they've led all beings to enlightenment, in actual fact, these bodhisattvas don't forsake their own enlightenment. The significance of their vow is that if it were beneficial for others, they would gladly forsake their own liberation. However, because they realize they'll be more efficacious in helping others as a Buddha, they actively seek enlightenment. Once they become Buddhas, they'll still manifest in the world to guide others.

In Mahayana Buddhist texts, Buddhahood, or full enlightenment, is a step beyond the lofty attainments of arhats. One way to distinguish the two is according to the level of obscurations removed from their minds.

There are two levels of obscurations. The first is the afflictive obscurations, which are afflictions and karma. The second level is the cognitive obscurations, which are the imprints of the afflictions and the appearance of phenomena as inherently existent. These obscurations prevent us from being omniscient or directly perceiving all phenomena simultaneously. The two levels of obscurations are analogous to onions in a pot and the smell remaining once the onions have been removed. When the afflictive obscurations have been removed, one attains liberation or arhatship. If one continues to purify the mind, removing the cognitive obscurations, one attains the complete enlightenment of a Buddha.

Because a bodhisattva aspires to help others in the most effective and extensive way, he or she meditates to purify both obscurations. While lower level bodhisattvas still have afflictive obscurations, the higher bodhisattvas have eliminated them and are in the process of removing their cognitive obscurations. When a bodhisattva becomes a Buddha, he or she can then manifest in the world in whatever ways are necessary to lead others to enlightenment.

Some people become arhats first before becoming Buddhas, while others enter directly into the bodhisattva path. The former generate the firm determination to be free from cyclic existence, thereby entering the path of the hearers or solitary realizers. After attaining nirvana, they abide in a state of bliss. Later on, they cultivate the altruistic intention to attain enlightenment in order to benefit others. At this time, they enter the bodhisattva path and later attain Buddhahood.

Other people cultivate both the determination to be free and the altruistic intention from the beginning. When both of those are firm, they enter the bodhisattva path directly without first becoming arhats. At the end of the bodhisattva path, they too become Buddhas.

The Fourth Truth: The Paths to Cessation

Full cessation is the absence or stopping of all sufferings and all of their causes. To arrive at this freedom, we must follow the correct path. In the *Mahaparinirvana Sutra* and in many other sutras, the Buddha described the path to nirvana as the three higher trainings—ethical discipline *(shila)*, concentration *(samadhi)*, and wisdom *(panna, prajna)*. He also enumerated the noble eightfold path, which can be subsumed in the three higher trainings.

Higher Training in Ethical Discipline

The higher training in ethical discipline is the foundation of the practice. Through it, we cease doing negative actions that eventually cause us pain.

The application of ethical discipline is very practical for it improves the quality of our daily lives. As we cease harming others through negative actions, our regret and guilt will subside. In addition, others will trust us and will be attracted to us. We'll die peacefully, free from fear of being reborn in bad circumstances. All the positive potential (merit) we create by abandoning destructive actions and creating positive ones sets a firm foundation for all future realizations of the path.

Three branches of the noble eightfold path are included in the higher training in ethical discipline. Although they are briefly explained below, their meanings become clearer if we reflect on them by thinking of examples from our lives.

1. Right action. Acting properly, we can avoid creating the three destructive actions of the body: killing, stealing, and unwise sexual behavior.

Killing is intentionally taking the life of any being, including animals. The advice to avoid killing challenges us to think creatively of alternate means to resolve conflict besides violence.

Stealing is taking what isn't given to us. It includes not paying taxes or fees that are due, borrowing things and not returning them, and taking things from our workplace for our own personal use.

Unwise sexual behavior refers chiefly to adultery but in general includes any sexual behavior that physically, mentally, or emotionally harms ourselves or others.

Right action teaches us to be aware of the effects of our actions on others. Instead of doing whatever pleases us at the moment, we'll be considerate of others. Automatically, our relationships will improve and others will be happier in our company.

Right action also includes physically acting in ways that benefit others. This includes helping an elderly person to clean house, saving others' lives by rescuing them from danger, and so on.

2. Right speech. Right speech begins with avoiding four destructive actions of speech: lying, divisive words, harsh words, and idle talk.

Lying is verbally saying or indicating through a nod or a shrug something we know isn't true. However, telling the truth isn't an absolute standard and must be tempered with compassion. For instance, it isn't wise to tell the truth to a murderer about a potential victim's whereabouts, if this would cause the latter's death.

Divisive words is speech that causes others to quarrel or prevents them from reconciling once they've had a falling out.

Harsh words is any speech that hurts others: insult, abuse, ridicule, sarcasm, and so on. Sometimes harsh words can be said with a smile, as when we innocently pretend what we have said won't hurt another.

Idle talk is wasting our time and others' time talking about inconsequential topics only for amusement.

Through training in right speech, we'll communicate in ways pleasing to others. Our relationships with other people will be more fulfilling if we take care of what we say to them and how we say it. Rather than venting our anger or frustration onto another, we'll think about effective ways to communicate our needs and feelings to them. In addition, we'll make an effort to notice and comment upon others' good qualities and achievements. We'll give others moral support, console them in times of grief, and teach them the Dharma. Speech is a powerful tool to influence others and if we use it wisely, many people will benefit.

The Buddha advised us to avoid ten destructive actions: three physical, four verbal, and three mental. The three physical actions were discussed under right action and the four verbal under right speech. Avoiding the three destructive actions of mind—covetousness, maliciousness, and distorted views—aren't specifically mentioned under the higher training in ethical discipline, but they'll be discussed here because avoiding them helps us to live ethically.

Coveting others' possessions is when we plan how to procure something belonging to another person. While covetousness is a mental action no one else can see, it can lead us to flatter, bribe, cheat, or steal from others to obtain what we desire.

Maliciousness is planning to harm others. It includes thinking how to take revenge for a wrong done to us, how to hurt others' feelings, or how to embarrass them.

Holding distorted views involves vigorously and angrily denying the existence of such things as past and future lives, the possibility of attaining nirvana, the existence of the Buddha, Dharma, and Sangha. Doubt about these subjects doesn't constitute distorted views. However, if we neglect to resolve our doubts by asking questions and investigating these issues, we could later generate distorted views by believing in deceptive doctrines.

Deliberately refraining from these ten destructive actions is engaging in the ten constructive or positive actions. For example, deciding not to lie to our employer about the time spent working on a project is in itself a positive action. This has many benefits: Our employer will trust our word in the future, we will live according to our ethical principles, and we will create the cause to have temporal happiness and spiritual realizations in the future.

3. Right livelihood. Material possessions are needed to sustain our lives, but it's important to procure them in proper ways. It's detrimental to engage in any of the physical or verbal negative actions to earn a living. For this reason, the Buddha recommended that we avoid being a butcher, hunter, or soldier and avoid jobs that entail manufacturing or selling liquor, weapons, or poisonous substances. Similarly, let's seek employment that does not involve fraud or deceit.

Some people may wonder, for example, how people could eat if there were no butchers or if no pesticides were used on crops. The important point here is we ourselves abandon wrong livelihood. We can't control what other people do, nor can we alone decide our country's policies. When there is a choice, we should select a profession that doesn't harm others. When there is no choice, then we must do the best we can, given the situation. The most important factor is to abandon the wish to harm others.

For monastics, right livelihood means keeping their precepts, thereby being worthy of offerings made to them. Flattering others, dropping hints, putting on the pretense of being holy, and giving a small gift in order to receive offerings are incorrect ways for a monastic to receive the requisites for life—food, clothing, shelter, and medicine. Similarly, deceiving or cheating others, telling fortunes, or performing magic to earn money is wrong livelihood. Everyone—ordained or lay—should play a useful role in society and not harm others.

The various sets of precepts set out by the Buddha are included in the higher training of ethical discipline. They are described in the chapter entitled "Precepts: Directing Our Energy Positively."

Higher Training in Concentration

Concentration is an essential part of the path, for without it our minds are unable to remain firmly on virtuous objects. For example, when we meditate on love, we must first generate that attitude and then maintain it. In that way, it will be fully integrated in our minds. When we meditate on emptiness, we must first penetrate its meaning and then sustain that understanding. Transforming our minds through meditation is possible only when we can stop uncontrolled distracting thoughts.

The higher training in concentration leads to meditative quiescence (shamatha), the ability to hold our concentration on the meditation object for as long as we wish. In the process of developing meditative quiescence, a practitioner chooses one particular meditation object, for example, the breath or an image of the Buddha. Once meditative quiescence is attained, concentration can be directed at any object: emptiness, love, etc. With meditative quiescence, the mind and the body are extremely pliant, making meditation very easy and enjoyable.

The next three branches of the noble eightfold path are included in the higher training of concentration:

4. *Right effort.* To progress on the path, we need to put our energy into Dharma practice. This entails happily directing our effort toward purifying negative actions already done and preventing doing new ones in the future. Effort also is necessary to maintain the virtuous states we've already generated and to induce new ones in the future. Doing this definitely improves the quality of our lives.

5. *Right mindfulness.* Mindfulness is a mental factor that enables us to remember and to keep our attention on what is beneficial. For example, in the morning when we awake, we can determine, "Today I will try not to harm others and to benefit them as much as possible." Mindfulness enables us to keep this thought in our minds all day, making us aware whether or not our daily actions correspond to this motivation. Being mindful of the ten constructive actions enables us not to lie, steal, and so forth when we're tempted to do so.

Mindfulness is also important in meditation. Meditation means familiarizing ourselves with a beneficial object or attitude. For example, we may focus our attention on our breath as we inhale and exhale. This clears the flurry of thoughts from our minds, and eventually, we'll be able to concentrate single-pointedly on the breath. The meditation object may vary: in some meditations, we may focus on the breath, in others on a visualized image of the Buddha or on the attitude of loving-kindness for all beings.

To develop single-pointed concentration, or samadhi, we must eliminate all opposing states of mind such as forgetfulness, laxity, and agitation.

Forgetfulness prevents us from maintaining our object of meditation— the breath, the image of the Buddha, the kindness of other beings, and so on. We forget the object of meditation and are distracted by the flurry of thoughts in our minds.

Laxity occurs when the mind is dull and its clarity or attentiveness decreases. If we don't oppose gross laxity, we may fall asleep on our meditation cushion. If we neglect to remedy subtle laxity, we may wrongly believe we've attained a high level of concentration when we haven't.

Agitation interrupts the stability of our concentration. It distracts us from the meditation object by diverting our attention to something to which we're attached. For example, we may be trying to meditate when we find that our attention has drifted to food. Suddenly the bell rings to end the meditation session, and we realize we haven't meditated at all!

Mindfulness counteracts these hindrances. It is a mental factor that repeatedly returns our attention to a familiar object, in this case the meditation object—the breath, etc. It's important to learn how to meditate. Then, our mindfulness will be strong, and we won't forget the meditation object as easily. If we do, our introspective alertness will warn us that we're distracted. Renewing our mindfulness, we'll again bring our attention back to the meditation object.

Mindfulness makes our concentration stable, thus counteracting agitation. It also enables our minds to be clear and attentive, thus eliminating laxity. Through experimentation, we must find the correct balance between making our concentration too tight or too loose. Tightness causes agitation, and this disturbs the stability of our concentration. Loose attention brings laxity and disturbs the clarity and attentiveness of the mind. The balance between making our attention too loose or too tight is like fine-tuning a violin. The Indian meditator and sage Chandragomin said:

> If we do not make the effort to build intensive attention, the mind will begin to sink, and we will never be able to achieve clarity. On the other hand, if we place too much emphasis on maintaining intensive attention, this causes the mind to wander from the object, and we will never be able to achieve stability. Hence, it is not easy to keep to the middle way when developing a single-pointed mind.

In addition to employing the mental factor of mindfulness as an essential aid in developing concentration, the Buddha also spoke of cultivating mindfulness of four objects: our bodies, feelings, minds, and phenomena. Through this practice, we're able to realize three characteristics: that all products are constantly changing, that all things under the influence of disturbing thoughts and karma are miserable, and that all phenomena are selfless.

6. *Right concentration.* Our concentration or single-pointedness slowly improves through effort and mindfulness, until we attain meditative quies-

cence. We may also progress to deeper states of concentration, the actual meditative stabilizations *(jhana, dhyana)* of the form and formless realms.

These levels of meditative stabilization are cultivated by non-Buddhists as well. However, when a Buddhist cultivates them, his or her mind is sustained by refuge in the Three Jewels (Buddha, Dharma, and Sangha), and by the determination to be free of all sufferings of cyclic existence. Whereas non-Buddhists tend to be satisfied with the bliss of the various meditative stabilizations, Buddhists employ the meditative stabilizations to realize emptiness, thereby attaining liberation.

The Buddha gave extensive teachings on mindfulness and concentration. If you're interested in learning more, ask a spiritual mentor for instruction or refer to books on the subject.

Higher Training in Wisdom

Through living ethically, we'll eliminate physical and verbal negative actions. By developing concentration, the manifest afflictions will temporarily subside. However, without wisdom, there is no way to liberate ourselves from cyclic existence and attain lasting happiness. To eradicate the cause of all problems—ignorance—from our mindstreams, the wisdom realizing emptiness (generally synonymous with selflessness or lack of an inherent self) is necessary.

To gain this wisdom that realizes the deeper nature of how people and phenomena exist, we must practice special insight *(vipassana, vipashyana)*. Special insight is a discriminating wisdom conjoined with the pliancy of meditative quiescence and induced by the power of analysis.

Prior to the attainment of special insight, whenever analytical meditation is done, our concentration is disturbed, and whenever the mind concentrates single-pointedly, it's unable simultaneously to engage in analysis. However, when special insight is attained, concentration and analysis don't disturb each other, thereby making the mind very powerful. When special insight is directed toward selflessness, it cleanses our mindstreams of ignorance, afflictions, karma, and their imprints so that they never return.

To develop meditative quiescence and special insight, we must train for a long time. Like learning to read, developing concentration and wisdom takes time and continuous practice. In our modern times of push-button appliances and fast food, we tend to be impatient and expect ourselves to gain high realization without much effort. However, this isn't possible. A few people, those who have cultivated the path extensively in previous lives, may make rapid progress in this life. But for the majority of us, this isn't the case. Therefore, it's helpful if we have a long-range goal, patience, enthusiasm, and a happy mind that aspires to what is good.

The last two branches of the noble eightfold path are included in the higher training of wisdom:

7. Right view or understanding. This is the understanding of the four noble truths: the truths of suffering and its causes perpetuate cyclic existence; the truths of cessation and the path are the way to liberation. Specifically, right view is the wisdom that opposes deluded views—such as the concept that grasps our body-mind complex as having an inherent self—which keep us bound in cyclic existence. This will be discussed more in depth in the section on wisdom.

8. Right thought. Non-attachment, benevolence, and non-harmfulness are the characteristics of right thought. On a deeper level, right thought refers to the mind that subtly analyzes emptiness, thus leading us to perceive it directly.

3 FROM CONFUSION TO ENLIGHTENMENT: A STEP-BY-STEP METHOD TO TRANSFORM OUR MINDS

The four noble truths and the noble eightfold path are one way to explain the path. The gradual path to enlightenment is another. These two ways are compatible. It's helpful for us to know them both, for by looking at the same thing from different perspectives, our understanding increases.

Since the Buddha gave teachings to a wide variety of audiences, beginners are sometimes confused about where to start and how to progress. Therefore, in the early eleventh century, the Indian sage Atisha extracted the essential points from the sutras and ordered them into a gradual path. These are contained in his text *Lamp of the Path*. The Tibetan sage Lama Tsongkhapa (1357–1419) later expanded on the points in Atisha's text and wrote the *Great Exposition on the Gradual Path to Enlightenment*.

The gradual path gives us an overview of the entire process of moving from confusion to enlightenment. It sets out in a clear manner the steps to realize the path. If we're familiar with these steps, then whenever we hear a Dharma teaching we'll know what level of the path it applies to. By understanding the practices at different stages of the path, we'll realize there are no contradictions in Buddha's teachings. They can all be included in one person's practice to reach enlightenment. Knowing this, we'll avoid the great fault of criticizing any Buddhist tradition or teaching.

What follows is a summary of the gradual path to enlightenment. More extensive explanation can be received by attending talks or reading any of the excellent books on the subject.

Precious Human Life

The first step of the path is to realize our present opportunity to practice the Dharma and to attain the fruits of the practice. If a beggar doesn't realize she has a jewel in her pocket, she won't make use of it and will remain poor. Similarly, if we don't understand our great opportunity, we won't use our time wisely.

Currently, we have precious human lives with many advantageous qualities that not all beings have. Because of this, we can make our lives highly meaningful. We often take our lives for granted and dwell on the things that aren't going the way we would like them to. Thinking this way is unrealistic and makes us more and more depressed. However, if we think about the freedom and qualities we do have and everything that is going well, we'll have a different and more joyful perspective on life.

One of our greatest endowments is our human intelligence. This precious quality enables us to investigate the meaning of life and to practice the path to enlightenment. If all of our senses—eyes, ears, mental—are intact, we are able to hear the Dharma, read books on it, and think about its meaning. We're born in an historical era when the Buddha has appeared and taught the Dharma. These teachings have been transmitted in a pure form from teacher to student in lineages stemming back to the Buddha. We have the opportunity to meet qualified spiritual masters who can teach us, and there are communities of ordained people and Dharma friends who share our interest and encourage us on the path.

Those of us who are fortunate to live in countries that cherish religious freedom aren't restricted from learning and practicing the path. In addition, most of us don't live in desperate poverty and thus have enough food, clothing, and shelter to engage in spiritual practice without worrying about basic physiological needs. Our minds aren't heavily obscured with distorted views and we have interest in self-development.

We have the potential to do great things with our present opportunity. But to appreciate this, we must develop a long-term vision. Our present lives last only a short time. Our mindstreams don't cease when our physical bodies die. Our minds are formless entities, and when they leave our present bodies at the time of death, they will be reborn in other bodies. What rebirth we'll take depends on our present actions. Therefore, one purpose of our lives can be to prepare for death and future lives. In that way, we can die peacefully, knowing our minds will be propelled toward good rebirths.

The second way we can utilize our lives is to attain liberation or enlightenment. We can become arhats, beings liberated from cyclic existence, or we can go on to become fully enlightened Buddhas, able to benefit others most effectively. Attaining liberation, our minds will be completely cleansed of all afflictions. Thus we'll never become angry, jealous, or proud again. We'll never feel guilty, anxious, or depressed again, and all our bad habits will be gone. In addition, if we aspire to attain enlightenment for the benefit of everyone, we'll have spontaneous affection for all beings and will know the most appropriate ways to help them.

The third way to take advantage of our precious human lives is to live life to the fullest, moment by moment. There are several ways to do this. One is to be mindful of each moment, being in the here-and-now as we do each action. When we eat, we concentrate on eating, noting the taste and texture of the food. When we walk, we concentrate on the movements involved in walking, without letting our minds wander in distraction.

Another way to live each moment to the fullest is to practice thought transformation. For example, when we go up stairs, we can think, "May I lead all beings to fortunate rebirths, liberation, and enlightenment." While cleaning dishes or clothes, we think, "May I help all beings cleanse their minds of afflictions and obscurations." When we hand something to another person, we think, "May I be able to satisfy the needs of all beings." We can creatively transform each action by generating the wish to bring happiness to others. Other techniques for making our daily lives meaningful are explained in the chapter "Practical Guidelines for Good Living."

Three Levels of Motivation

Having decided to make our lives meaningful, we can progress along the paths of the three levels of training. These correspond to the three levels of spiritual seekers. In *Lamp of the Path,* the great Indian sage Atisha said:

> Those who fervently work by some means merely for happiness in cyclic existence are known as those of minimal spiritual motivation. Those who, having turned their backs on the pleasures of cyclic existence and with a nature turned from negativities, fervently work for just their own serenity (liberation) are known as people of intermediate motivation. Those who fully wish to elimi-

nate completely all the problems of others as they would the problems afflicting their own mindstreams are those of supreme spiritual motivation.

These three motivations and their corresponding trainings form the
gradual path. The first level is the foundation for the second, which is the
basis for the third. To progress along the path, we train serially, although we
may aspire for full enlightenment throughout. These three motivations and
their trainings in brief are:

1. The initial level. Here we want to prepare for death so we can die
peacefully and attain a good rebirth. To this end, we'll contemplate impermanence and death, the disadvantages of unfortunate rebirths. At this point,
our principal practice will be taking refuge in the Three Jewels and observing cause and effect (karma). Taking refuge is entrusting ourselves to the
spiritual guidance of the Buddhas, Dharma, and Sangha. Observing cause
and effect entails trying to avoid the ten destructive actions and to act
positively. Many of the practices of the higher training in ethical discipline
start at this point of the path, as do right action, right speech, and right
livelihood.

2. The intermediate level. Here we seek to be completely free from
the cycle of rebirth. To this end, we'll contemplate the sufferings of cyclic
existence in general and the problems of each type of rebirth in particular.
We'll also consider the role of afflictions and karma in keeping us bound in
cyclic existence. In this way, we'll generate a firm determination to be free
from all difficulties of cyclic existence and to attain liberation. Our principal practice will be the three higher trainings, especially concentration and
wisdom. All the branches of the noble eightfold path will be practiced as
well.

3. The highest level. Here we seek liberation not only for ourselves
but for all beings. To do this, we must generate *bodhichitta*, the altruistic
intention to attain enlightenment in order to benefit all beings. Thus, we'll
meditate on great love, great compassion, and altruism. Seeing the full enlightenment of the Buddhas as the best way to help others, we'll engage in
the bodhisattvas' practice of the six far-reaching attitudes (perfections,
paramitas): generosity, ethical discipline, patience, joyous effort, meditative stabilization, and wisdom. Vajrayana practice then enables us to attain
the body and mind of a Buddha.

Let's now begin with the initial level to learn how to gradually transform our minds.

THE FIRST STEP: PREPARING FOR THE FUTURE

Remembering Death

The opportunity our precious human lives provide doesn't last forever. Death comes to everyone. Most people feel uncomfortable thinking about death, fearing that talking about death will bring it closer. However, by their very nature our lives are impermanent, and death is inevitable. Given that death is an irrevocable result of living, it's good to think about it to make our lives more meaningful.

Regarding death from a proper perspective can give us direction and energy to live fully. It's also a powerful tool for subduing our afflictions and making our minds peaceful, for when we recognize we'll inevitably die, all the petty concerns that worry us become insignificant compared to the importance of practicing the path before our lives end. The Buddha said:

> There is no greater realization than awareness of the impermanence of our lives. Just as the elephant's footprint is the biggest of all animals' footprints, so is meditation on impermanence the most powerful meditation.

At the time of death, our mindstreams and the imprints of the actions we've created go on to future lives. If we spend our precious human lives doing harmful actions with bad motivations, the imprints of those actions will come with us. In addition, since we've reinforced our anger, jealousy, and other negative emotions, they'll be stronger in future lives.

On the other hand, if we use our time wisely to cultivate positive states of mind—generosity, patience, love, compassion, concentration, wisdom— then the imprints from the actions they've motivated come with us. Also, those beneficial attitudes are stronger and can arise more easily in future lives. Thus, it's important to be concerned about what we think, say, and do right now.

Death definitely comes to everyone. Whether we're rich or poor, famous or humble, we'll die. No one can live forever, for our bodies naturally decay and die. There is nowhere we can go to avoid death. Our life spans can't be extended and with every passing moment, they're becoming shorter. Death comes, whether or not we've taken the time to practice the path. When our life spans run out, we can't bargain for more time in order to transform our minds. Truly realizing the certainty of death, we'll make a firm decision to practice the Dharma.

The time of death isn't certain. The duration of our life spans isn't fixed, and even though statistics give a general indication of how long people live, that's not a guarantee about our own lives. It's incorrect to think we'll die when our life's work is complete, for people are always in the middle of doing something when they die: Some people leave for vacation and don't return; some begin a meal and don't finish it.

Sustaining our lives takes great effort. If we simply did nothing, we'd naturally die. To stay alive, we have to arrange for food, shelter, clothing, medicine, and other necessities. Even some things that are supposed to sustain life terminate it: For example, a house kills the people in it during an earthquake; bad food causes fatal illnesses. Our human bodies are very fragile. The skin is easily penetrated, the bones so easy to break. Even tiny viruses cause the demise of huge humans. Deeply understanding the un-certainty of the time of death, we'll determine to practice the Dharma now, without procrastinating.

At the time of death, we must leave all our possessions behind. Al-though we spend our lives amassing things, not one of them can accom-pany us at death. Likewise, our friends and relatives can't come with us. Although we deeply care about them, at death there is no choice but to separate. Even our bodies, the one thing we've had since the beginning of this life, are left behind at death. Only our karmic imprints accompany our mindstreams to future lives. Only our Dharma practice can benefit us at death. Genuinely understanding this, we'll determine to practice Dharma purely, without worldly motivations seeking wealth or reputation.

Does this mean Buddhists can't have fun and must live austerely? No, it doesn't. Let's ask ourselves, "What is really beneficial in life?" We must examine the motivations behind our actions and the results they'll bring in future lives. In this way, we can decide what is beneficial to do.

For example, if we cheat in business to increase our profits so our family can live in luxury, our motivation is a selfish one. Although we want our relatives to be happy, we're placing their happiness above that of the people we're cheating. In fact, both parties want happiness and equally deserve a good life. If we act negatively, out of partiality for our own family, we harm others. Although our families may have a few extra possessions, at the time of death those stay behind, and the negative imprints we created by cheating others accompany us to future lives.

Understanding this, we'll see that the disadvantages of cheating outweigh its benefits, and we'll avoid doing it. Our families may have slightly fewer possessions, but we'll be able to sleep with a clear conscience. The positive action of deliberately avoiding cheating will bring us good results in the future.

Let's take another example: Idle talk is usually considered a destructive action because it wastes our time. But if our friend is depressed and can't listen to wise advice, we can joke, tell silly stories, and use small talk to lighten his mood. Because our motivation is kind, our joking and chatting are positive.

Laughing and having a good time aren't in opposition to Dharma. The more we leave behind attachment, anger, jealousy, and pride, the more we'll enjoy whatever we're doing. Our hearts will open to others and we can laugh and smile with ease. The holy beings I've been fortunate to meet have a wonderful sense of humor and are very friendly.

In Buddhist groups, it's important for people to get to know each other and have a sense of fellowship. We can share experiences with our Dharma friends and encourage each other on the path. Buddhism isn't an isolated path, and it's important for Buddhists to cultivate group unity and companionship.

It's not beneficial to retreat inside ourselves, thinking, "Every time I talk to someone I'm motivated by attachment. Therefore, I'll concentrate on meditation and chanting and won't socialize with others." One of the fundamental principles of Buddhism is care and compassion for others. Although at times we may need to distance ourselves from others in order to settle our own minds, whenever possible we should actively develop genuine love for others. To do this, we must be aware of what's happening in others' lives, care about them as we do ourselves, and offer help whenever possible. Our ability to act with love develops with time and practice, and it has to be balanced with our need for private contemplation.

Buddhism isn't opposed to having material possessions, keeping our bodies healthy and attractive, or caring for our friends and relatives. Our possessions, body, or dear ones don't enslave us. The real problem lies with our attachment, anger, and other afflictions that arise in relation to these things. If we're attached to material possessions, then we're likely to lie, cheat, or steal to get them. Or we may stingily cling to our possessions or use them selfishly to gain fame or to exert power over others. This attachment binds us, affecting not only our relationships with others in the present but our rebirths in the future.

On the other hand, we can think, "I need certain possessions to sustain my life and my family. I'll work honestly to get them and will share them with others and use them to spread the Dharma." With such a motivation, we'll live ethically and will create positive potential—positive karmic imprints on our minds—by being generous. In addition, we'll be more relaxed because we'll be free from miserliness.

The Danger of an Unfortunate Rebirth

After death, where will we be reborn? From a Buddhist point of view, this depends upon our actions while alive and which imprints mature at the time of death. If we're angry at the time of death or if we cling strongly to our possessions and dear ones, that will encourage the ripening of negative imprints, which will propel us toward a rebirth full of problems. If we die thinking of the Three Jewels or dedicating our lives for the benefit of others, that will facilitate the ripening of positive imprints to propel us toward a fortunate rebirth.

In cyclic existence there are six realms: the fortunate ones are the realms of the gods, demi-gods, and humans; and the unfortunate ones are the realms of hellish beings, hungry ghosts, and animals. It may seem strange to think that we can be born in these other life forms, but if we examine our minds, we'll see that it's possible.

For example, sometimes we humans act and think like animals or even worse. We can be greedy, territorial, ferocious, or dull-witted like some animals. While animals only kill to eat or to defend themselves, sometimes humans kill out of whim, spite, or desire. If humans act like that, it seems natural that at the time of death their minds will be attracted toward bodies that match their mental states.

Unfortunate rebirths aren't punishments for acting badly. The compassionate Buddha didn't create these realms, nor does he judge us and send us to them. These realms are creations of our own minds, and the imprints of our actions direct us toward them. The Indian sage Shantideva said:

The immense fires and burning iron ground
Of the hellish realms
Are not somebody's creation
But arise from the destructive thoughts within our minds.

All the horrors that exist on the earth
Arise from the evil minds of beings.
Thus, if we can conquer the craziness of our minds,
We will have conquered all of cyclic existence.

In this and previous lives, we've done many actions—some harmful and some beneficial—and these imprints remain on our mindstreams. Dreading the unfortunate rebirth those imprints could bring, we'll seek help to prevent it. Having confidence that the Three Jewels can guide us to happiness leads us to seek refuge in them.

Taking Refuge

Taking refuge is entrusting ourselves to the guidance of the Three Jewels—the Buddhas, Dharma, and Sangha. By knowing the qualities of the Three Jewels and their ability to guide us from the danger of unfortunate rebirths and show us the path to happiness, we'll trust their instructions.

Buddhas are those beings who have completely removed all afflictions, karma, and obscurations from their mindstreams. They also have fully developed their good qualities. Thus, Buddhas have the compassion, wisdom, and skillful means to indicate to us the path to happiness that they themselves followed.

Those beings who are now Buddhas haven't always been enlightened. They were once caught in the net of cyclic existence, plagued by their attachment, anger, and ignorance, just as we are. However, by practicing the path, they purified their minds and developed their qualities, thus attaining enlightenment, the state of perfection. We can do the same if we follow the instructions they gave from their own experience.

Shakyamuni Buddha is often referred to as "the Buddha." He lived 2,500 years ago and is the Buddha of this historical period. However, there are many Buddhas, and we can turn to all of them for refuge. Some Buddhas reside in pure lands, those places created by the power of their positive potential and enlightening influence. Buddhas can also manifest as beings in our world in whatever forms are suitable to guide us. They don't identify themselves but instead appear as ordinary beings. Through their behavior or their teachings they guide us on the path.

The Buddhas are fully qualified guides because they have completely gone beyond cyclic existence. Therefore, their wisdom, compassion, and skill in helping others aren't limited. Worldly deities, such as those born in the godlike realms, are still subject to death and rebirth under the influence of afflictions and karma and thus aren't able to guide us to liberation.

In addition, Buddhas have skillful means by which they lead us. There are numerous stories in the Buddhist scriptures (sutras) of extremely ignorant, angry, or attached people whom the Buddha was able to lead to liberation.

Buddhas have great compassion and thus definitely will help us. In addition, they are impartial and thus guide us no matter how we treat them in return. Buddhas don't play favorites like ordinary beings. Nor are they offended by others' criticism or flattered by their praise.

The Buddhas' help extends to all beings equally, just as the rays of the sun radiate in all directions. However, sunshine can't enter a covered pot. Similarly, the Buddhas' enlightening influence can't reach the minds of beings with many obscurations and little positive potential. If the pot is later uncovered, the sun's rays enter easily. Thus, it's important for us to eliminate our obscurations and make our minds as receptive to the Buddhas' influence as we can.

The Dharma refuge is the last two of the four noble truths: true cessations and true paths. That is, Dharma is the realizations of the path and the absence of suffering and its causes. These exist in the mindstreams of those who have directly realized emptiness. In a more general sense, Dharma refers to the Buddha's teachings.

It's said that the Dharma is the real refuge. This means the realizations (clear understandings) and cessations (stopping of suffering and its causes) that we gain are our real protection. The Buddhas give the teachings and show the way; the Sangha provide an example and help us to practice. But our own realizations will directly stop our pain and confusion.

The Sangha refuge refers to those persons—ordained or lay—who have direct perception of emptiness. These include arhats, as well as the hearers, solitary realizers, and bodhisattvas who have realized emptiness directly. Because they perceive reality as it is, they can help us do the same.

In a more general sense, Sangha refers to the communities of monks and nuns who have dedicated their lives to practicing the path, although the individuals themselves may or may not have realizations. Individual monastics are dedicated to following the path, but it's not correct for us to expect them to be perfect beings yet.

Buddhist deities such as Avalokiteshvara (Kuan Yin), Manjushri, and others may be regarded as Buddhas or as bodhisattva Sangha. We can view them in a variety of ways. In one way, they are historical beings, and we can read their biographies in the sutras. Regarding them in this way, we're inspired by the examples of their lives and are encouraged to practice as they did.

Another way to regard these deities is as manifestations of magnificent qualities. Thus, it is said that Avalokiteshvara is the manifestation of compassion, and Manjushri is the emanation of the wisdom of all the Buddhas. Both Avalokiteshvara and Manjushri have the same realizations, for the omniscient minds of all Buddhas have the same qualities and know the same things. However, in this case, Avalokiteshvara and Manjushri are seen as symbols of specific qualities.

Sometimes it's difficult for us to conceive of great compassion for all beings. But when this quality is symbolically and artistically represented, we can understand it better. With one thousand arms outstretched to help others and one thousand eyes to see their needs, the physical appearance of Avalokiteshvara reminds us of compassion. Thus, we meditate on Avalokiteshvara to develop all enlightened realizations, especially compassion.

Once someone has become a Buddha, he or she (in actual fact a Buddha has no gender) may appear in the form of any of the deities. Thus, the omniscient mind of one Buddha can simultaneously appear in the form of Avalokiteshvara to benefit some people, in the form of Manjushri to benefit others, as our Dharma teacher, as an animal, or even as an inanimate object like a bridge. Once someone's mindstream is fully purified and developed, it has the ability to appear in a wide variety of forms to benefit others and lead them to enlightenment.

We may view the deities in yet a third way: as our own Buddha-potential in its future, fully developed form. In this way, when we turn to the Buddha for guidance, we remind ourselves that the Buddha we'll become is the one who ultimately will protect us from suffering. This encourages us to remember and develop the Buddha-potential existing within ourselves right now.

An analogy illustrates how to relate to the Three Jewels. We are like a sick person, afflicted by sufferings and their causes. The Buddha is the doctor who diagnoses and prescribes medicine. The Dharma is the medicine, and the Sangha are the nurses who help us take it. In this way, we'll be cured and will be well and happy.

Karma: The Law of Cause and Effect

The first medicine the Buddha prescribed for us is to observe karma, i.e., to abandon destructive actions and create positive ones. Thus, he explained the ten destructive actions, which were described in the previous chapter. Karma was also discussed in the chapter "Mind Is the Creator of Our Experience."

There are four principal characteristics of karma:

1. Karma is definite. When we plant apple seeds, apples grow, not oranges. Similarly, when we act positively, happiness follows, never suffering. When we act destructively, misery comes, never happiness.

2. Karma is expandable. Just as a small seed can grow into a huge tree with much fruit, small actions can bring large results. Therefore, let's try to avoid even small negative actions and to create small positive ones.

3. If the cause isn't created, the result doesn't occur. If no seed is planted, nothing grows. The person who hasn't created the cause to be killed won't be even if she is in a car crash. Likewise, if we don't create the cause to realize the path, we won't realize it. Mere praying to the Buddha won't bring the effect we wish if we do nothing to create the principal cause. People who pray for wealth and yet are miserly are like those who pray to pass their exams but don't study. We must create the appropriate causes for something to occur. Prayer then stimulates the cause to mature.

4. Karma doesn't get lost. If we do positive actions, the happy result will eventually come. When we do negative actions, the imprints aren't lost even though they may not bring their results immediately.

Through study and contemplation, we can gain a clear understanding of the functioning of karma. Although we can't go beyond the bounds of cause and effect, there is flexibility within it. Karma isn't cast in concrete and can be changed. For example, if we get angry or have distorted views, we impede our positive karma from ripening. If we purify negative imprints from our minds, we can impede or completely prevent them from maturing.

Thus, it's wise for us to engage in the four opponent powers to purify negative karma:

1. **Regret our destructive actions.** With wisdom, we recognize and admit our errors. Regret is different from guilt, for the latter immobilizes us emotionally and is an exaggeration of our afflictions. Regret, on the other hand, comes from an honest assessment of our actions and enables us to learn from our mistakes.

2. **Take refuge and generate the altruistic intention.** We act destructively in relation to either holy beings or ordinary beings. By taking refuge in the Three Jewels, we restore our relationship with the holy beings; and by generating love, compassion, and altruism, we restore our relationship with ordinary beings.

3. **Determine not to do those negative actions in the future.** The stronger our determination, the easier it will be to avoid habitually acting destructively.

4. **Engage in a remedial practice.** In general, this could be any virtuous action: helping those in need; offering service in our community; listening, reflecting, or meditating on the Dharma; bowing or making offerings to the Three Jewels; printing Dharma books; and so on.

This concludes the initial step. It describes the practice of someone who seeks good future rebirths: taking refuge in the Three Jewels and observing the law of cause and effect by avoiding destructive actions and creating constructive ones.

THE SECOND STEP: THE WISH FOR FREEDOM

Practitioners of the initial level prepare to be able to die peacefully and to have a happy rebirth. Although this may appear to be future-oriented and to ignore happiness in the present, in fact the opposite is true. By being concerned with future lives, we'll be more aware of what is happening in the present, because our present actions create our future experiences.

Also, to avoid harmful actions, we'll endeavor to subdue the attachment, anger, and confusion that cause them. If we do this, our minds will be freer to live in the present without the worries, anxieties, and distractions caused by afflictions. Paradoxically, concern for future lives leads us to live more in the present.

After a while, we may begin to think, "Even though my rebirths will be fortunate, still I'm caught in cyclic existence. Is this a satisfactory situation?"

Good rebirths are temporary measures to prevent the suffering of unfortunate ones. But we're still subjected to birth, sickness, aging, and death without choice. There is no lasting security in any rebirth, for each of them, even the most wonderful ones, comes to an end. Controlled by afflictions we go up and down, from one rebirth with its problems to the next with new problems.

Understanding this, a determination will grow within us to be free from all rebirths. Wishing to leave cyclic existence behind, we'll aspire for liberation, a state of lasting peace founded on wisdom. To attain this, we'll strive to develop the concentrated wisdom that can cut the root ignorance.

The four noble truths and noble eightfold path are generally discussed under the middle level. As these have been discussed previously, only a summary of the middle level is presented here. However, the four noble truths and noble eightfold path aren't restricted to the intermediate scope. For example, right action, speech, and livelihood are the basic practice of a person on the initial level.

Contemplating the four noble truths leads us to generate the determination to be free from cyclic existence. The three higher trainings are the essential practice leading to liberation. The wisdom aspect of the three higher trainings will be explained in a subsequent section of this chapter.

The Third Step: Seeking Enlightenment for the Benefit of All

At the initial level of spiritual practice, people prepare for death and future lives. This makes sense to them, and they're capable of doing this. After a while, when their understanding increases, they realize that good rebirths alone won't bring lasting happiness. Their goals expand, and they want to be completely free from the cycle of uncontrolled rebirth. They now become practitioners of the intermediate level and seek liberation.

Later, they may again reassess their goals, and ask, "Is my own attainment of liberation sufficient? What about everyone else?" They now develop a strong sense of universal responsibility for the welfare of all others. Thus, they develop bodhichitta: the altruistic intention to attain enlightenment in order to benefit all beings.

The Altruistic Intention

The Buddha taught two methods to cultivate the altruistic intention. One is the seven points of cause and result, which was emphasized by the sages Maitreya and Asanga. The other is exchanging self and others. This was elaborated on by the Indian master Shantideva. For the sake of brevity, only the seven points of cause and effect will be discussed here.

Before cultivating the seven points of cause and effect, it's necessary to develop equanimity, an equal feeling toward all beings that is free from attachment to our friends, aversion to enemies, and apathetic indifference toward strangers. (Here "enemy" means anyone with whom we don't get along or who makes us uneasy.)

As long as we rigidly discriminate people as friends, enemies, and strangers, it's impossible for us to develop impartial love for each of them. Therefore, equanimity not only pacifies confused emotions toward others but is also the basis for cultivating genuine love and compassion for them.

Attachment, hostility, and indifference toward others arise when we only regard their immediate, superficial characteristics. For example, today Sue gives us a present and Joe gossips about us so we consider Sue our friend and Joe our enemy. Tomorrow Joe gives us a gift and Sue talks behind our back. Suddenly our feelings change, and Joe is a friend and Sue is an enemy.

In fact, both Sue and Joe have acted similarly, so how can we say one is a real friend and the other a real enemy? If we look beyond their superficial actions, we would see that both have good qualities and both have weaknesses. Thus, having attachment to one because he or she is "good" and aversion for the other who is "bad" is an unrealistic response.

In addition, our relationships with them as friend, enemy, or stranger are temporary. When we were born, Sue and Joe were strangers and we were indifferent to them. Sue then became our friend and later our enemy, while for Joe it was the opposite. These relationships are likely to change again, with Sue becoming a friend or a stranger, and Joe becoming our enemy again or even a stranger.

Throughout our previous lives, everyone has been a friend, enemy, or stranger at some time. Our relationships with others are in constant flux. Therefore, attachment, hostility, or indifference to them is inappropriate. The Buddha said:

Those who at present hold a hostile attitude toward us have been our beloved mother, father, friend, brother, and sister countless times. Those who benefit us now have also been our bitter enemy. Therefore, we should cast away any kind of resentment toward those who harm us, cast away attachment to those we like, and thus extend a loving mind toward all beings equally.

Recognizing that no person is our inherent, ever-lasting friend, enemy, or stranger releases us from the confused emotions of attachment, hostility, and indifference. This in turn will create in us an equal feeling of openness and concern for each person. We'll no longer feel alienated from some people or fearful that others will desert us.

From the basis of equanimity, we can proceed to develop the altruistic intention through the seven points of cause and effect. There are six causes:

1. Recognizing that all beings have been our mother
2. Remembering our mothers' kindness
3. Wishing to repay it
4. Love
5. Compassion
6. Great determination

These six result in the seventh point, the altruistic intention of bodhichitta.

Recognizing That All Others Have Been Our Mother

The first step is to recognize that all beings have been our mother. In this meditation, our mother is chosen because in general people feel close to their mothers. However, if we have a difficult relationship with our mother, we may choose our father, grandparents, or whoever was very kind to us when we were young.

Recognizing that the countless sentient beings have all been our mother challenges us to go beyond the confines of our present way of thinking. First, we must have some feeling that rebirth exists, that who we are now is one in a series of lives without beginning.

Because it may seem difficult to recognize we haven't always been who we are now, it's helpful to think of the changes that occur in one lifetime.

Imagine how differently we felt as infants: our bodies were different; our perception of the world was different. It almost feels as if those infants were different people, unrelated to the capable adults we are now.

If we envision ourselves as ninety years old, it seems as if that forgetful and bent-over old person is unrelated to us. However, the infant, our present self, and the wrinkled and senile old person exist in one continuity. We can be all of them.

Similarly, our minds can exist in a variety of other bodies. We've had many previous lives. Thus, we've had many mothers who have given birth to us and raised us during those lives. Our present mother hasn't always been our mother, for in previous lives we may have been born in one place and she in another. Thus, many beings have been our mothers in previous lives.

Since we have had an infinite number of previous lives, all beings at one time or another have been our mother. Because our minds are obscured by ignorance, we can't remember their having been our mother, and because we have taken new bodies, we don't recognize them in this life. However, if we remind ourselves that all beings have been our mothers, then whenever we see someone, there will be a spontaneous feeling of closeness.

For example, let's say when we were young, we were accidentally separated from our parents, whom we loved very much. Thirty years later, we walk down the street and see two beggars. At first we ignore them or are even hostile toward them. Then we look again, and suddenly we realize they are our parents. They look different and so do we, so at first we don't recognize each other. But when we do, we suddenly feel an extraordinary concern and love for those beggars. We have no reservation about helping them. It's similar with training ourselves to recognize that all beings have been our parents in previous lives.

Remembering Others' Kindness Toward Us

The second step is to remember the kindness and care that others have shown us. To do this, we initially take the example of our present mother or whoever cared for us when we were young.

Our mother carried us in her womb for nine months, even though being pregnant was very uncomfortable. She endured the pain of giving birth to us, cared for us when we were helpless infants, and put up with our childish temper tantrums and bad behavior. Although our mother probably didn't like to discipline us, she had to in order to teach us ethical discipline and manners, thus enabling us to get along with others. She taught us to speak and made sure we had a good education. Within our parents' financial limits, they bought us toys and took us on trips.

Some people find it uncomfortable to think about the kindness of their parents. They may feel that since they didn't ask to be born, they don't owe their parents anything. Some people resent their parents because their parents disciplined them severely, denied them things that other children had, or even abused them.

If we feel this way, then reflect on the kindness of whoever helped us when we were young. Later, we may wish to learn the techniques the Buddha taught for reducing anger and developing patience and apply these to our relationship with our parents. It's important to remember that whatever negative feelings our parents had toward us or us toward them, they did provide us with our body and make our precious human life possible. Whatever their motives were, they cared for us to the extent to which they were physically and mentally capable. If we can appreciate this and forgive them for their weaknesses, our hearts will open toward them. Please see the chapter "Parent and Child" for more discussion of this.

The purpose of remembering our mother's kindness isn't to generate attachment for her, because attachment is a disturbing attitude. Rather, we want to honestly recognize her kindness as this enables deep gratitude to arise in our minds. We then generalize this heart-warming gratitude to all beings by remembering that they all have been our mothers in the past and have been as kind to us as our present mothers. This gratitude will lead us to the third step, wishing to repay their kindness.

Wanting to Repay Others' Kindness

When we recognize others' kindness, automatically we want to do something in return. This isn't a feeling of burdensome obligation toward others but rather a spontaneous joy and concern for others.

Love

From this wish to repay their kindness, we'll go on to think how wonderful it would be if all those kind people could have happiness. This is love: the wish for them to be happy and to have the causes of happiness. Since we have previously freed ourselves from attachment to friends, aversion to enemies, and apathetic indifference to strangers, our love will be impartial and will extend to everyone equally. We'll love others simply because they exist, with no strings attached. The Tibetan sage Lama Tsongkhapa said:

> From our point of view, all beings are equal to us because they have all been our beloved mothers, fathers, brothers, sisters, and friends countless times. From that point of view, all beings should also be treated as equal to us because they equally desire happiness and shun unhappiness. Therefore, we should try to maintain a loving mind toward all beings equally.

Compassion

When we consider the problems and pain that others undergo, we'll then generate compassion: the wish for others to be freed from all suffering and its causes. Compassion is different from pity and other condescending attitudes. Compassion recognizes ourselves and others as equal in terms of wanting happiness and wanting to be free from misery. It enables us to help them with as much ease as we now help ourselves.

The Great Determination

Having deep compassion, we progress to the sixth step, assuming the responsibility to bring others happiness and to free them from suffering. Whereas previously we wanted others to be happy and to be free from misery, now we're determined to do something about it.

The Altruistic Intention, Bodhichitta

But how can we lead others to happiness when we're confused ourselves? One drowning person can't save another; similarly, one person caught in the web of cyclic existence can't show another the way out. To guide others, we must know their karmic predispositions, their inclinations, and interests. We also must know all the teachings in order to teach others what is suitable for them.

Thus, to actualize our wish to lead others from suffering and to happiness, we need to have perfect compassion, wisdom, and skillful means. As only a Buddha has these qualities, we must attain enlightenment to benefit others in the most effective way. This aspiration for enlightenment is bodhichitta, the altruistic intention. When we become so familiar with this attitude that it is our spontaneous reaction to all others, then we become bodhisattvas, the spiritual children of the Buddhas. Because of this noble and magnificent attitude, our ability to help others now and in the future increases tremendously.

The Far-Reaching Attitudes: Active Compassion

After generating the altruistic heart, the next step is to practice the six far-reaching attitudes that lead to enlightenment. Sometimes called the six perfections or the six paramitas, they are generosity, ethical discipline, patience, joyous effort, meditative stabilization, and wisdom.

Practicing generosity, ethical discipline, and patience with joyous effort directly benefits others now. But the final aim of all six far-reaching attitudes is to actualize the wisdom directly perceiving emptiness. Through this wisdom, we will then eliminate all afflictions and remove all stains and obscurations from our mindstreams, thus becoming fully enlightened Buddhas. At this point, our ability to help others will be totally developed.

Although these six are practiced throughout the path, at this point they're called far-reaching attitudes because we engage in them motivated by the altruistic intention and because they are sealed by contemplating the emptiness of their components—the agent, object, and action. In this way, they lead to the development of full wisdom, thus enabling us to reach far beyond cyclic existence. Thus, it's important for us to engage in the six far-reaching attitudes with an altruistic motivation, contemplate emptiness while we're practicing them, and dedicate the positive potential created to the enlightenment of all beings.

Far-Reaching Generosity

The first far-reaching attitude, generosity, is the willingness to give whatever we have to help others. This practice counteracts the miserliness and laziness that often arise when others approach us for help. There are three types of far-reaching generosity:

1. Giving material possessions
2. Protecting others in danger and sorrow
3. Counseling others and teaching them the Dharma

Most of us ordinary beings tend to be miserly and more concerned with protecting our own property than with making others happy by being generous. Often we fear that by giving something, we'll suffer from not having it. We give only as much as we have to in order not to lose face. Generally, we keep the best for ourselves and give whatever is left to others. After giving, we remind others how much we've done so they'll feel obliged to help us in return.

These miserly motivations create tension in our minds and prevent us from creating positive potential and gaining spiritual realizations. Miserliness is a selfish state of mind that considers our own happiness more important than that of others. As long as we're miserly, we're never satisfied no matter how much we have.

When miserliness makes us hesitant to give, we can remember that our wealth is impermanent and that one day we'll have to separate from it. There's no sense in clinging to it. If we use it by sharing it with others, we'll counteract the miserliness that causes unfortunate rebirths. If we train ourselves to feel joy in giving, our generosity will bring happiness to others and to ourselves.

Generosity isn't a matter of guiltily telling ourselves we "should" give. It's developing a heart that finds genuine joy in making others happy. This doesn't mean we should give everything away so that we have nothing and become a burden to those around us. Rather, we give according to our means. The amount isn't as important as the motivation.

It's crucial to give wisely. Offering an alcoholic a drink isn't charity; giving money for the purchase of weapons, poison, and illegal drugs doesn't benefit anyone. We shouldn't harm some beings in order to give to others. Thus, it's not wise to kill animals or ask others to kill them so our family can have a nice meal.

It's best if we help people who are helpless, desperate, poor, or sick. Also, making offerings to sincere Dharma practitioners supplies them with the daily necessities to continue their practice. When we offer to the Three Jewels, we support Dharma activities, construction of temples and facilities, publication of books, and social services provided by temples.

The second type of generosity, giving protection, involves helping those who are suffering or in danger. This could include saving a drowning child, helping sick or old people who are neglected, working to prevent cruelty to animals, constructing hospices for the dying, and helping those with AIDS or cancer to receive proper medical attention. When there are earthquakes, floods, and other natural disasters, we should help in whatever way we can.

Giving guidance and teachings, the third type of generosity, includes many activities. We can console those who are grieving or in difficulty. It's also beneficial to encourage others not to lie or cheat and to act in constructive ways. By doing so, we show others the way to have more peace of mind now and to create the cause for future happiness. Chanting prayers so the sick or dying can hear them and turn their minds toward virtuous thoughts is also beneficial.

The best gift to give others is the Dharma. To do this, we instruct and encourage them on the path to enlightenment. This gives others the means to release themselves from all suffering and to attain lasting happiness.

Far-Reaching Ethical Discipline

The far-reaching attitude of ethical discipline is safeguarding our body, speech, and mind from negative actions. Ethical discipline is extremely important, for without it we can't attain higher realizations.

Not understanding this, some people chant or meditate but are careless about their behavior in daily life. They seem very holy when they're doing rites and rituals, but afterward they take intoxicants, gossip, and engage in shady business deals. Wanting to keep one foot in cyclic existence and the other in nirvana, these people don't progress on the path. The great Indian scholar and practitioner Atisha said:

> Most of us think that the practice of Dharma is to recite some commitment, visualize a deity, or chant. But real Dharma practice is the integration of positive activities into our lives. If we are aware of this, we might gain more realizations in our daily lives than during our sitting meditations.

Far-reaching ethical discipline is of three types:

1. Abandoning destructive actions
2. Engaging in constructive actions
3. Leading others to live ethically

By abandoning the ten destructive actions and keeping whatever precepts we've taken, we free ourselves from the gross level of afflictions that propel us to act negatively. Thus, our minds automatically become calmer, less distracted, and free from regret. This enables us to concentrate better during meditation.

By acting constructively, we enrich our minds with positive potential and benefit others. By our example and by our instructions, we can then lead others to act ethically.

Far-Reaching Patience

Patience is inner calm and strength that enables us to act clearly in any difficult situation. There are three types of far-reaching patience:

1. Not retaliating when we are harmed
2. Transcending problems and pain with a positive attitude
3. Enduring difficulties encountered in Dharma practice

The first type of patience enables us to be clear-minded and peaceful no matter how others treat us. At present, when we receive harm, we often blame the other person and become agitated. Sometimes our agitation takes the form of self-pity and depression, and we complain about how badly others treat us. Other times, it becomes anger and we retaliate by harming the other person.

Patience acts as an antidote to this because it views the situation from a different perspective. As long as we're in cyclic existence, we're sure to meet people who cause us problems. This is the nature of our existence. But patience helps us have a broad perspective on the situation: Because we created negative actions in the past, now we experience the consequences.

Thus, rather than seeing the other person as the principal cause of our pain, we recognize that our own afflictions and negative actions are the real source. Instead of harming other people, we put more energy into overcoming our afflictions and purifying our negative actions.

When people harm us, they're generally doing so because they're unhappy. If we truly understand this, we can stop being preoccupied with our own situation and consider the unhappiness of those who harm us. We know what it's like to be miserable, which is how they're feeling. Thinking in this way, we can transform those who harm us into objects of our compassion.

We know that sometimes our afflictions take control of us, causing us to do and say harmful things. Similarly, people who harm us are under the influence of their own anger and jealousy. Just as we want people to forgive our shortcomings, so too do others wish us to be tolerant and not take what they say and do personally when their emotions get out of control.

Being patient doesn't mean being passive or cowardly and thus letting others do whatever they want. Rather, we need to free our own minds from anger first and then look at the situation clearly. We can then try to do whatever is most beneficial for everyone in the situation, which may involve being firm and preventing someone from harming others.

The patience to transcend problems enables us to transform painful situations, such as sickness and poverty, into supports for our Dharma practice. Rather than becoming depressed or angry when we're plagued with difficulties, we'll learn from these experiences and face them with courage. Experiencing difficulties makes us more compassionate toward those in similar situations. Our pride is deflated, our understanding of cause and effect increases, and we won't hesitate to help someone in need.

Patience is a necessary quality when practicing Dharma, and developing this is the third type of patience. Sometimes it's difficult to understand the teachings, to control our minds, or to discipline ourselves to meditate daily. Patience helps us overcome this and to wrestle with our unruly minds. Rather than expecting instant results from practicing briefly, we'll have the patience to cultivate our minds continuously, over years.

Far-Reaching Joyous Effort

Joyous effort is essential if we are to make continual progress in the Dharma. If we lack enthusiasm, many hindrances arise, chiefly in the form of laziness. Laziness is of three kinds:

1. If we're attached to sleep and relaxation, we procrastinate and never get around to practicing.
2. If we're attached to worldly activities, we're too busy to study, contemplate, and meditate.
3. If we're discouraged and lack self-confidence, we forsake our practice.

Joyous effort is the antidote to these three types of laziness. For instance, by remembering the transience of our lives and the certainty of death, our overindulgence in sleep will vanish. The preciousness of our human life will become clearer, and we'll want to use it wisely before we die.

Of course we have to sleep to be healthy, but too much sleep makes our minds dull and wastes our time. When we die, we'll have nothing to show for all the extra hours we spent lying around. However, if we use our time wisely to practice, our deaths will be peaceful and we'll have many good qualities and virtuous imprints to carry with us to future lives. As Shantideva said:

Relying upon the boat of a human (body),
Free yourself from the great river of pain (cyclic existence);
As it is hard to find this boat again,
This is no time for sleep, you fool!

From a Buddhist perspective, busying ourselves with worldly activities is a form of laziness, because we're lax in self-cultivation. Our lives are so busy in modern society: Our appointment books are completely full and we're always running here and there. We often complain there isn't enough time for the Dharma.

However, whenever we have a spare moment, we work overtime or call some friends to fill in the gap. We always have time to eat, but we hardly ever have time to nourish ourselves spiritually by attending Dharma classes or meditating. When the temple has entertainment and free meals, we go; but when there is meditation or lessons, we're busy.

This hindrance to spiritual progress comes because we're attached to worldly pleasures: food, money, reputation, amusement, and friends. The harm comes from our inappropriate way of relating to them. Attached, we selfishly indulge in them. However, these things in and of themselves aren't bad. Through pacifying our afflictions, we can enjoy these things with a good motivation—to improve ourselves for the benefit of others.

By remembering the truth of suffering, we'll realize there's no lasting joy to be found in worldly pleasures. Enjoying them is like drinking salt water: Rather than satisfying us, they make us crave for more. Similarly, no matter how much money we have, we never have enough; no matter how many times we go out drinking and to the movies, we still are dissatisfied; no matter how high we are on the corporate ladder, there's always someone who is higher.

Being attached to these things only keeps us ensnared in dissatisfaction in this life and in constantly recurring problems in future lives. By reminding ourselves of this, we'll practice the Dharma enthusiastically and won't get sidetracked by senseless activities. As Lama Tsongkhapa said:

There is no satisfaction in enjoying worldly pleasures. They are the door to all misery. Having realized that the fault of cyclic existence's perfections is that they cannot be trusted, may I be strongly intent on the bliss of liberation—inspire me thus!

This doesn't mean we become Dharma fanatics and refuse to talk with others or do our work. That is another extreme. What we're seeking is a balance whereby we cultivate a good motivation for all activities we do and leave aside useless activities that waste our time and lead us to act negatively.

The third type of laziness is discouragement: We may think that we're incompetent, that the bodhisattva path is too difficult, or that the goal of enlightenment is beyond our reach. This way of thinking makes our minds spiral downward into depression. Feeling hopeless, we abandon our efforts at practice.

It's important to remember we always have within us Buddha-nature—the potential to become a fully enlightened Buddha. This potential is our birthright and can never be taken away. If we practice the path—eliminating our obscurations and developing our good qualities—Buddhahood is assured. Shantideva paraphrased the *Subahupariprccha Sutra* and added his own comment:

The *tathagata*s (Buddhas) who speak what is true
Have uttered this truth:

"If they develop the strength of their exertion,
Even those who are flies, mosquitoes, bees, and insects
Will win the unsurpassable enlightenment
Which is so hard to find."

So, if I do not forsake the bodhisattvas' way of life,
Why should someone like myself who has been born in the human race
Not attain enlightenment, since I am able to recognize
What is beneficial and what is of harm?

Far-Reaching Meditative Stabilization

Many of the important points about meditative stabilization were discussed earlier under the higher training in concentration. As was noted, non-Buddhists also develop concentration and can gain clairvoyant powers due to their practice. However, when Buddhists practice meditative stabilization, it's supported by refuge in the Three Jewels and the determination to be free from cyclic existence. Thus, when Buddhists join together the meditative stabilizations of meditative quiescence and penetrative insight into emptiness, they will attain liberation. In addition, when they develop the altruistic aspiration for enlightenment, their meditative stabilization will lead to full enlightenment, or Buddhahood.

Because the motivation with which we engage in meditation determines what the result of our practice will be, it's important to take refuge in the Three Jewels and develop a virtuous aspiration at the beginning of every meditation session. To help us do this, we can recite the following prayers:

I take refuge in the Buddhas,
I take refuge in the Dharma,
I take refuge in the Sangha.

I take refuge until I am enlightened in the Buddhas, the Dharma, and the Sangha. By the positive potential I create by practicing generosity and the other far-reaching attitudes, may I attain Buddhahood in order to benefit all sentient beings.

May all beings have happiness and its causes.
May all beings be free from suffering and its causes.
May all beings not be separated from sorrowless bliss.
May all beings abide in equanimity, free from bias, attachment, and
    anger.

These prayers help to prepare our minds for meditation. Having generated a good motivation at the beginning, we'll have less distraction during the actual meditation session. Our meditation object could be the breath, the four foundations of mindfulness, love and compassion, visualization and recitation of mantra, or analytic meditation in which we think about a subject the Buddha taught.

At the conclusion of the session, we dedicate the positive potential created during our meditation for the benefit of all beings. Sometimes dedication is translated "transference of merits," which is a confusing term in English. Dedicating our positive potential doesn't mean it is transferred to another person's consciousness like money is transferred from one bank to another, for this would contradict the law of cause and effect. When we create positive potential and dedicate it to the well-being of others, it acts as a cooperative condition, enabling their own good karmic imprints to mature.

Dedication safeguards our positive potential from being destroyed if we later become angry or have distorted views. It also prevents us from being attached to our own spiritual achievements. We can dedicate as follows:

Due to this positive potential, may I soon attain the enlightened state of a Buddha, so that I may be able to liberate all beings from their sufferings.

Far-Reaching Wisdom

Far-reaching wisdom is of three types:

1. The wisdom understanding that emptiness of inherent existence is the ultimate nature of all phenomena
2. The wisdom understanding conventional phenomena, for example, the functioning of cause and effect, grammar, logic, science, the arts, and so forth
3. The wisdom knowing how to benefit others

Since the first wisdom—that which realizes emptiness—is the key to liberation and enlightenment, it will be discussed here. Emptiness is a profound subject, and it's best to study with a qualified master to understand it fully. What follows is only an introduction to the subject.

There are many advantages to developing the wisdom realizing emptiness. This specific type of wisdom is the sole means to eliminate our ignorance and other afflictions. It is also the most powerful tool for purifying negative karmic imprints. In addition, it enables us to benefit others effectively, for we can then teach them the correct meaning of emptiness.

Ignorance prevents us from perceiving how we and other phenomena exist. It also misconceives how things exist, projecting a false way of existence onto them. By realizing that things are free from the fantasized projections we put on them, we prevent afflictions from arising. An example will make this clear.

We can become very emotional about money. If we see a large amount, we often become excited and start to think of everything we could buy if that money were ours. If we lose our money, we're worried and upset, for something of value is gone.

It appears to us that the money has an inherent worth: In and of itself it's important. It seems that the money and its value exist inside those bills, independent of anything else. We need only look at our reaction if someone burns a large bill to see that we spontaneously feel the money is inherently valuable.

Let's look again. What is money? It's paper with ink designs on it. That's all. On the basis of paper printed with certain designs, we add value and importance. In and of itself, the paper is worthless. Only because we assign the label "money" to those pieces of paper do they become currency. Only because as a society we give value to this currency does it have worth.

The money, as well as its value, exists because our minds attribute names and meaning to those printed pieces of paper. That is, the money exists due to the power of our concepts about those pieces of paper. In actual fact, the money is empty of inherent or independent existence. This is because it exists dependently: It depends on its causes (for example, the trees from which the paper came), its parts (front, back, right, left), and our minds that label it "money" and attach value to it.

Why is it important to understand that money is empty of inherent existence and yet exists dependently? Because this awareness will prevent us from overestimating its importance. If we don't understand emptiness, then we can develop many disturbing ideas and reactions to money. For example, some people are obsessed by it; others aren't satisfied no matter how much they have; some become proud and flaunt their wealth; others quarrel and even injure people to get money.

If we understand that money is a creation of our society, dependent upon our conceptual minds as well as upon the printed paper, then we'll have more realistic attitudes toward it.

Similarly, all phenomena and persons exist by depending on other factors: prior causes and conditions, their constituent parts, and the conceptual minds that label them. This is the meaning of "dependent arising."

Thus, emptiness and dependent arising complement each other. Things are empty because they lack inherent or independent existence; their existence depends on other factors.

People and phenomena don't have inherent or independent existence, nor are they totally non-existent. The meaning of emptiness and dependent arising falls between these two extremes: This is the view of the middle way taught by the Buddha. Lama Tsongkhapa said in the *Three Principles of the Path*:

> In addition, appearances clear away the extreme of (inherent) existence; emptiness clears away the extreme of non-existence. When you understand the arising of cause and effect from the viewpoint of emptiness, you are not captivated by either of the extreme views.

The first step toward the realization of emptiness is listening to teachings and studying books on the subject. Then we think about what we've learned and discuss it with others to eliminate our wrong ideas. Third, we meditate, integrating what we've understood with our mindstreams.

Two elements are important in the meditation on emptiness. The first is meditative quiescence, the ability to keep our mind single-pointedly on the meditation object, in this case emptiness. The second is special insight, the wisdom factor that correctly analyzes and discerns emptiness. Actual special insight is combined with meditative quiescence.

By repeatedly meditating on emptiness, we totally dispel all wrong conceptions and afflictions from our mindstreams. Because our meditation is motivated by the altruistic intention, it will result in enlightenment.

4 PRACTICAL GUIDELINES FOR GOOD LIVING

Taking refuge in the Buddha, Dharma, and Sangha helps us to focus on what is important in our lives. It gives our lives a positive direction and reaffirms our conviction that there exists a path to happiness.

When taking refuge, we're enriched by the knowledge that great beings with full compassion, wisdom, and skillful means exist. We gain confidence that by following the path, we'll attain the same state they have. Refuge is also a way of fulfilling a promise we've made to ourselves—a promise to become better people and make a positive contribution to others' welfare.

The real taking refuge occurs deep in our hearts and isn't dependent on doing or saying anything. Nevertheless, we may wish to participate in the refuge ceremony by requesting a monk or nun to formally give us refuge. The refuge ceremony is brief: we repeat a passage after our teacher and open our hearts to make a strong connection with the Three Jewels of the Buddha, Dharma, and Sangha. The ceremony also "officially" makes us a Buddhist.

The reason we take refuge is to prevent future suffering and to progress along the path. To be true to our goals, we must act according to this motivation after taking refuge. The Buddha gave guidelines for us to follow so we can continually improve ourselves.

It's not the case that after we take refuge we're "saved," and thereafter can do anything we please. Taking refuge is the first step in giving our lives a positive direction, and we must continue to channel our energy in that direction. Therefore, the Buddha gave advice on how to practice to ensure we remain true to our determination to improve. The points in which to train ourselves are:

1. In keeping with taking refuge in the Buddha, we should commit ourselves whole-heartedly to a qualified spiritual master. Whoever performed the refuge ceremony for us becomes one of our spiritual mentors. We may have more than one teacher, and it's good to make strong prayers to meet fully qualified mentors with whom we feel a close Dharma connection. It's beneficial if we follow the Dharma instructions our teachers give us, care for our teachers, and treat them with respect.

2.   In keeping with taking refuge in the Dharma, we practice listening to and studying the teachings, as well as putting them into practice in our daily lives. Some people think only monastics study the teachings deeply, and such dedicated study and practice is too difficult for lay followers. This is incorrect. Everyone should listen to and study the teachings as much as possible. If we want to progress along the path, we must practice the Dharma. Receiving instructions is essential in order to practice.

3. In keeping with taking refuge in the Sangha, we respect the Sangha as our spiritual companions and follow their good example. If we constantly look for others' weaknesses, that's all we'll see. Such an attitude prevents us from appreciating whatever good qualities they have and learning from them. We shouldn't expect monastics to be perfect. Although they have dedicated their lives to the path, it takes time to gain realizations, and most of the Sangha are endeavoring to pacify their afflictions and karma, just as we are. Shaving one's head doesn't make one enlightened. However, we can appreciate their effort to practice purely, and the good example they set for us. Although individual monastics may have faults, we can still respect the fact they have taken the vows set forth by the Buddha.

4. We try to train ourselves in accordance with the examples set by the Buddha, Dharma, and Sangha. If we take their behavior as a model, we'll eventually become like them. When we're in a state of emotional turmoil, it's helpful to ask ourselves, "How would a bodhisattva respond to this situation?" Thinking about this, we'll consider other ways to handle our problem.

5. We practice avoiding being self-indulgent, running after any desirable object we see. Craving money and status leads us to obsession and constant dissatisfaction. We will be much happier if we enjoy pleasures of the senses in moderation. Similarly, let's avoid arrogantly criticizing whatever we dislike. It's so easy to see others' faults and overlook our own. Yet

this doesn't make us or others any happier. It would be more constructive to correct our own faults than to point out those of others.

6. As much as possible we try to avoid the ten destructive actions and keep precepts. We can take the five lay precepts for the duration of our lives, or we can take the eight precepts for one day. Ethical discipline is the foundation of the practice; without ethical discipline, there is no way to create the cause for good rebirths or to attain realizations.

7. We train ourselves to develop a compassionate and sympathetic heart toward all other beings. To do this, it's helpful to meditate continually on love, compassion, and altruism. If we don't contemplate patience before meeting a troublesome person, it will be difficult to control our temper. We need to prepare beforehand, by remembering the kindness of others and continually meditating on patience in our daily meditation sessions. Chapter 6 of Shantideva's *Guide to the Bodhisattva's Way of Life* is effective in helping us learn the antidotes to anger. If we nurture patience in our meditation, then when we go to work or school, we'll be mindful and will notice when we're getting angry. At that time, we will be able to remember what we've contemplated in the meditation sessions and let go of our anger. We won't always succeed, but over time we'll notice progress. Each evening it's helpful to review our day. If we discover any remaining anger in our minds, it's helpful to again reflect on patience and the altruistic intention.

8. On Buddhist festival days, it's advisable for us to make special offerings to the Three Jewels to accumulate positive potential.

Points 5–7 emphasize the importance of improving our relations with others. Following Buddha's teachings doesn't mean performing rites and rituals to gain a superficial feeling of being "holy." It means not harming others and helping them as much as possible in our daily lives.

Specific Guidelines

To help us develop and maintain a good relationship with each of the Three Jewels individually, there are guidelines specific to refuge in the Buddha, Dharma, and Sangha:

Refuge in the Buddha

Having taken refuge in the Buddha, who has purified all defilements and developed all qualities, we do not turn for refuge to worldly gods who lack the capacity to guide us from all problems. Although some worldly gods have psychic powers, they aren't free from cyclic existence. Taking ultimate refuge in them is like one drowning person asking another to take him to shore.

We should respect all images of the Buddha and avoid putting them in low or dirty places, stepping over them, or pointing our feet toward them. Because the statues represent the noble state we want to attain, we take care of them. The statues don't need our respect, but we need to be mindful of the Buddha's qualities that they represent.

The purpose of Buddha statues is to help us remember the enlightened state and work toward attaining it ourselves. Therefore, we do not use religious objects as collateral for a loan or buy and sell them as someone buys and sells used cars—with the motivation to earn a living. The profit made from selling statues or Dharma books should be used to purchase or produce more Dharma items, not to buy ourselves a good meal or new clothes.

When looking at various images, it is nonsensical to discriminate, "This Buddha is beautiful, but this one isn't." How can a Buddha be ugly? We can comment on the artist's skills in making a statue or painting, but not on the looks of a Buddha.

Also, don't treat expensive statues with respect while neglecting those that are damaged or less costly. Some people put the expensive beautifully made statues in the front of their shrines so their friends will say, "You have such lovely and costly things in your home!" Seeking praise for owning religious objects is a worldly attitude, and we might as well show off our VCR or bank book if all we're looking for is others' admiration.

Refuge in the Dharma

Having taken refuge in the Dharma, we avoid harming any living being. One becomes a Buddha in order to benefit others, and Buddhas cherish others more than themselves. Therefore, if we admire the Buddhas, we should respect all living beings just as they do.

Also, we respect the written words that describe the path to enlightenment by keeping the texts clean and in a high place. Avoid stepping over them, putting them on the floor, or throwing them in the rubbish when they are old. Old Dharma materials can be burned.

The reason for this is not that the paper and ink of the books are holy in and of themselves but that these books show the path to enlightenment that we want to develop in our minds. They are our spiritual nourishment.

We don't put our food on the floor without something underneath it, because the floor is dirty and we value our food. Similarly, if we remember the importance of Dharma books, which nourish us spiritually, we'll treat them properly. These guidelines make us more mindful of how we relate to things in our environment.

Refuge in the Sangha

Having taken refuge in the Sangha, we avoid becoming close friends with people who criticize the Buddha, Dharma, and Sangha, or who are unruly or harm others. We avoid these people not because they're "evil and bad," but because our own minds are weak. For example, although we may want to stop gossiping, if we're constantly in the company of people who gossip, we'll easily resume our old habits.

However, we shouldn't criticize or be rude to these people. We can have compassion for them, but we won't seek their company. For example, if a colleague is critical of our religious practice, we can be courteous and kind to him at work, but we won't go out with him after work or discuss religion with him. However, if someone is open-minded and wants to discuss religion in order to understand life, we can freely share our ideas and reflections with him.

The bodhisattvas and practitioners approaching arhatship, who don't run the risk of falling back into their old negative behaviors, seek the company of unruly beings in order to help them. However, if our practice isn't yet firm, we have to be careful of the environment in which we put ourselves.

Also, we cultivate respect for monastics as people who are earnestly endeavoring to actualize the teachings. Admiring their good qualities helps our minds, because it opens us to appreciate their qualities and learn from their examples. By respecting even the robes of ordained beings, we'll be happy and inspired when seeing them.

Common Guidelines

To help us deepen our refuge and extend it to others, there are six guidelines common to all the Three Jewels:

1. Mindful of the qualities of the Three Jewels and the differences between them and other possible refuges, we repeatedly take refuge in the

Buddha, Dharma, and Sangha. The qualities of the Three Jewels are explained in many texts. If we study these, our understanding of how the Three Jewels guide and protect us will increase. Taking refuge isn't done just once. Rather, it's a process through which we continually deepen our trust in the Three Jewels.

2. Remembering the kindness of the Three Jewels, we make offerings to them. Some people make offerings thinking that they're paying the Three Jewels back for what they've done or are obliging them to render help in the future. These people go to the temple and pray, "Buddha, if you make my sick relative recover and make my business flourish, I'll make offerings to you each year on this day." This is not the correct attitude to have when making offerings. We aren't doing business with the Buddha with the attitude, "Buddha, you deliver what I want, then I'll pay you." Offerings should be made with a good motivation, to eliminate our miserliness and to increase our joy in giving.

Some people make offerings as if they were in the business of earning merit. They regard merit as spiritual money and strive to collect it with a greedy mind. This is also an incorrect attitude. While it's beneficial to create positive potential, it's important to dedicate it for the welfare of everyone.

It's good to offer our food before eating. This enables us to stop and reflect for a moment rather than gobbling our food down with desire the way hungry animals do. To offer our food, we think, "Food is like medicine that cures the suffering of hunger. I must preserve my life so that I can practice the Dharma and be of service to others. Food is the fuel that allows me to do so. Many beings were involved in growing, transporting, and preparing this food. They were very kind, and to repay this I want to make my life meaningful. I can do this by offering the food to the Buddha with the motivation to become a Buddha myself in order to benefit all sentient beings most effectively."

Then imagine the food as pure and sweet wisdom-nectar that gives great bliss. Visualize a small Buddha made of light at your heart center and offer this nectar to him or her. To consecrate it, recite OM AH HUM three times. This is a mantra representing the qualities of the Buddha's body, speech, and mind. Then recite the following verses:

I now take this food, without greed or repulsion,
Nor merely for health, not for pleasure or comfort,

But simply as a medicine to strengthen my body
To attain enlightenment for the benefit of all.

The supreme teacher, the precious Buddha;
The supreme refuge, the holy precious Dharma;
The supreme guide, the precious Sangha:
To all of the objects of refuge I make this offering.

May we and all those around us
Never be separated from the Three Jewels in any of our lives.
May we always have the opportunity to make offerings to them,
And may we continuously receive their blessings and inspiration to
    progress along the path.

While doing this, we can close our eyes for a few moments, or if we're in a public place, we can visualize and say the prayers silently with our eyes open.

3. Mindful of the compassion of the Three Jewels, we encourage others to take refuge in them. When we recall how the Buddhas practiced the path and how the Sangha is practicing the path to help us, their compassion toward us becomes obvious. With their vast kindness, they teach us the Dharma, guide us, set a good example for us, and inspire us.

Aware of the benefit that taking refuge and following the Dharma has had on our own lives, we'll want to share this fortune with others. However, pressuring people to come to teachings or forcing our beliefs on others is both unskillful and rude. Let's avoid a football team mentality, thinking, "My religion is better than yours. I'm going to win more converts than you." We aren't in competition with other religions.

Nor do we go to the other extreme, keeping all Buddhist activities quiet, not publicizing them at all. If no one had organized and publicized Buddhist teachings, I never would have met the Dharma. I'm grateful to those who created the opportunity for me to contact and practice the Buddha's teachings.

Similarly, we can let others know about Buddhist teachings and activities and encourage them to come if they wish. To people who have no interest in Buddhism per se, we can express the meaning of the teachings in ordinary language. After all, much of Buddhism is common sense. For instance, we can talk to others about the faults of anger and how to calm hatred without using any Buddhist vocabulary. We can explain the disadvantages of selfishness and the advantages of kindness toward others in ordinary language.

In addition, others will notice our behavior and will wonder how we're able to remain calm and happy in bad circumstances. We needn't speak one word of Dharma to them, but by our actions they'll see the benefits of Dharma practice and will be curious about what we do. Some of my relatives once said to me, "You didn't get angry when that person criticized you!" After that, they became more open to learning about Buddhism.

4. Remembering the benefits of taking refuge, we take refuge three times in the morning and three times in the evening, by reciting and reflecting upon any of the refuge prayers.

It's extremely beneficial to start our day off in a positive way. When the alarm clock rings, let's try to make our first thoughts, "How fortunate I am to be alive and to have the opportunity to practice Dharma. The Three Jewels are reliable guides to lead me along the path to enlightenment. The best way to take the essence from my life is to develop the attitude of cherishing others and wanting to benefit them. Therefore, today as much as possible I'll avoid harming others and will be kind and help them."

Then we can recite three times the prayer for taking refuge and generating the altruistic intention:

> I take refuge until I am enlightened in the Buddhas, the Dharma, and the Sangha. By the positive potential I create by practicing generosity and the other far-reaching attitudes (ethical discipline, patience, joyous effort, meditative stabilization, and wisdom), may I attain Buddhahood in order to benefit all sentient beings.

It takes only a few moments to think in this way and to recite the prayer, yet doing so has a significant effect on the rest of our day. We'll be more cheerful and will be sure of our direction in life. Especially if we don't do a regular meditation practice, starting the day in this way is extremely beneficial.

In the evening, after reviewing the day's activities and freeing our minds from any remaining afflictions that may have arisen during the day, we again take refuge and generate the altruistic intention.

Before going to sleep, we can envision the Buddha, made of light, on our pillow. Placing our head in his lap, we fall asleep amidst the gentle glow of his wisdom and compassion.

5. We try to do all actions by entrusting ourselves to the Three Jewels. When we're nervous, it's good to visualize the Buddha, make requests, and imagine that light radiates from the Buddha and enters our body, filling it completely. If we're in danger, we can make prayers and request the Three Jewels for help and guidance.

Entrusting ourselves to the Three Jewels also refers to remembering their instructions. For example, when we're becoming angry, we can recall the techniques to cultivate patience. When we feel jealous, we can instead rejoice in others' happiness and good qualities. Our Dharma practice is our best refuge, for with it we'll develop the beneficial and correct attitudes that erase our problems.

6. We shouldn't forsake our refuge if our lives are threatened or for a joke. Whether we're happy or sad, maintaining confidence in and a good relationship with the Three Jewels is important. Some people become so distracted when enjoying pleasures of the senses that they forget their Dharma practice. Others become so discouraged when misfortune strikes that they forget the Three Jewels. Forgetting our refuge is harmful, for in doing so, we betray our own inner resolve to make our lives useful. By knowing that the Three Jewels are our best friends who will never abandon us, we'll always keep them in our hearts, no matter what external conditions we encounter.

All the above guidelines were set forth to help us make our lives meaningful. They are attitudes and actions in which we gradually train ourselves. It's wasted energy to feel we're guilty or bad because we don't follow these guidelines perfectly right now. Such self-judgment immobilizes us.

Instead, we can learn the guidelines and try to implement them as much as we can, reviewing them periodically to refresh our minds. We may choose one guideline to emphasize this week in our daily lives. Next week, we can add another, and so on. In that way, we'll slowly build up the good habits of practicing all of them.

5 PRECEPTS: DIRECTING OUR ENERGY POSITIVELY

To help us direct our actions, words, and thoughts positively, the Buddha outlined the ten destructive and the ten constructive actions (i.e., avoiding the ten destructive ones). In addition, he set up three sets of vows or precepts. The first level of precepts is the precepts for individual liberation. These help us to restrain from doing destructive physical and verbal actions. The second level of precepts is the bodhisattva precepts, which help us to subdue our self-centeredness. The tantric precepts constitute the third level, and they work against the appearance and conception of things being ordinary and self-existent.

Precepts or vows are a joy, not a burden. They aren't designed to keep us from having a good time or to make us feel deprived. The purpose of taking precepts is to give us internal strength so we won't act in ways that we don't want to. Having understood that killing, stealing, selfishness, and so forth only lead us to harm ourselves and others now and in the future, we'll want to avoid these. Taking precepts gives us energy and strength to do so. Therefore, it's said that precepts are the ornaments of the wise.

Precepts for Individual Liberation

To help people overcome their afflictions and stop committing harmful actions, the Buddha set out five precepts. During a brief ceremony performed by a monk or nun, we can take refuge in the Three Jewels—Buddha, Dharma and Sangha. At the same time, we can take any or all of the five lay precepts, and become an *upasaka* (male) or *upasika* (female).

The five precepts, which are taken for the duration of our life, are to avoid:

69

1. Taking the life of any being (killing)
2. Taking what is not given (stealing)
3. Unwise sexual behavior
4. Lying
5. Taking intoxicants

When giving refuge, some teachers allow us decide whether or not to take any or all of the precepts. Other teachers give all five precepts at the time of giving refuge.

The first four actions have been described in the chapter "The Four Noble Truths." The fifth precept is to abandon alcohol and intoxicating drugs. These substances are harmful because under their influence we lose the ability to discriminate right and wrong. Under the influence of alcohol and drugs, people say cruel things to others and even beat their spouses and children.

Some people hesitate to take this precept for they worry about social occasions when everyone is expected to drink. I wonder how many people at a party or business function really want to drink. Maybe each one is doing it because he or she thinks that everyone else expects them to, while in fact no one wants to!

Actually, it's not hard to refuse alcohol. Everyone in the room won't stop and stare at us because we don't drink alcoholic beverages! In fact, we may be a good example for others who are too dependent on alcohol. In any case, whenever we act according to our principles, we needn't be ashamed.

There are different interpretations regarding tobacco. In the Theravadin tradition smoking isn't prohibited by this precept, while in the Mahayana it is.

Coffee and tea may be taken. Although they have caffeine, they don't cause us to lose our senses. We can also take chili and other spices.

Lay practitioners also may take eight precepts for a period of 24 hours. The first time we take these precepts, we must take them from someone else who has the lineage of the precepts, that is, who has taken the precepts from his or her master, who in turn has taken them from his or her master. In this way, the continuity of the precepts can be traced back to the Buddha.

Having first taken the eight precepts from a qualified teacher, we can thereafter take them ourselves by imagining that we take them before all the Buddhas, bodhisattvas and arhats. The ceremony is brief and must begin before dawn. The precepts last until dawn of the following day.

Many people like to take the eight precepts on new and full moon days or on Buddhist festivals, although they may be taken on any day. The first five of these eight are similar to the five lay precepts, with the exception that the precept against unwise sexual behavior becomes sexual abstinence, because the precepts are kept for only one day.

The sixth precept is to avoid wearing perfume, ornaments, and cosmetics as well as to refrain from singing, dancing, and playing music. This precept helps us avoid distractions to our practice. If we sing and hum, then when we sit down to meditate, the tunes keep running through our minds. Not beautifying our body encourages us to cultivate our internal beauty of love, compassion, and wisdom.

The seventh precept is not to sit or sleep on a high or expensive bed or throne, as this could make us feel proud and superior to others.

The eighth precept is not to eat solid food after noon and to be vegetarian for the day. When some teachers give the eight precepts they say only lunch may be eaten, while other teachers allow both breakfast and lunch. Some teachers permit only water to be taken in the evening, others allow tea with a little milk, or fruit juice without pulp. The purpose of this precept is to reduce attachment to food. It also enables us to meditate better in the evenings, for if we eat a big supper, often we feel heavy and sleepy.

Taking precepts has incredible benefit. Just think of how different our environment would be if everyone took just the first precept, not to kill! The world would be a completely different place due to one precept. When we live with precepts, the lives of the people around us are immediately and dramatically affected: they live securely because of our firm intention not to harm them.

In addition, precepts make us increasingly aware of our actions, words, and attitudes. They enable us to know ourselves better because we'll become aware of our habitual actions.

Also, having decided beforehand what actions we want to avoid, we don't get into a wishy-washy state of mind when we find ourselves in a situation in which we're tempted to do something we know we'll regret later.

Every moment that we are not actively transgressing a precept, we accumulate great positive potential, even if we're sleeping. The reason for this is that we have made a firm decision not to do that action and are actively not doing it. This accumulation of positive potential forms a firm base for attaining spiritual realizations, and creates the causal energy for us to die peacefully and have a fortunate rebirth.

If people would like to become even more mindful of their actions of body and speech, they may take the *shramanera* (male) or *shramanerika* (female) precepts. These are ten in number, although the Tibetan tradition spells out all their sub-classifications, making thirty-six in all. Often called the novice ordination, it's taken for life, and one becomes a monk or a nun.

After taking the novice ordination, monks and nuns may take the full ordination, becoming a *bhikshu* (male) or *bhikshuni* (female). The number of vows varies among different Buddhist lineages, and within each lineage, the bhikshus and bhikshunis have different numbers of vows.

Traditionally, after taking the novice precepts and before taking the bhikshuni precepts, women take an intermediate ordination called *shiksamana* that adds six or twelve more precepts onto those taken as a novice, depending on the Vinaya tradition. Having held this ordination for two years, women may then take the full ordination. The lineages of these ordinations have been passed down—from teacher to student—without interruption from the time of the Buddha until today.

In the Theravadin countries of Southeast Asia, however, the nuns' ordination died out several centuries ago. Today there are women in Sri Lanka with ten precepts called *dasasilmata*s. In Thailand there are women entitled *maeji*s with eight precepts. But in both cases their precepts are considered to be lay precepts, and they aren't officially regarded as ordained nuns. However, many women are looking into the possibility of bringing the shramanerika, shiksamana, and bhikshuni lineages from the Chinese tradition back into the Theravadin tradition. In recent years some women from Sri Lanka have received the bhikshuni precepts.

In Tibet, the novice ordination for women took root, but the bhikshuni ordination didn't. While the shramanerika ordination can be given by four bhikshus or four bhikshunis, ten bhikshunis and ten bhikshus are required to give the bhikshuni ordination. It was difficult for women in those times to travel over the Himalayan Mountains, and thus the bhikshuni ordination didn't come to Tibet.

Chinese, Korean, and Vietnamese Buddhists still continue the lineages for both the bhikshu and bhikshuni ordinations. Some women from the Theravadin and Tibetan traditions have received bhikshuni ordination from

Chinese, Korean, or Vietnamese masters in recent years. People are now considering the possibility of reintroducing the bhikshuni ordination into the Theravadin and Tibetan traditions.

In Japan, the monastic precepts were altered during the Meiji Restoration in the mid-nineteenth century because the government wanted the ordained ones to marry. Thus, in Japan there are now both married and unmarried temple priests of both sexes, and the precepts they keep are enumerated differently from those of other Buddhist traditions.

Except for the eight precepts that are taken for one day, all other precepts are taken for the duration of one's life. It may happen that due to unforeseen circumstances a monk or a nun may not be able to keep the ordination any longer or may not wish to have it. In that case, he or she can go before a spiritual master, or even tell another person who can hear and understand, and return the precepts.

In Thailand there is a custom whereby at least once during their lives most men become monks and hold the precepts for three months. They usually do this when they are young adults, as it gives them a foundation in strict ethical discipline and is very auspicious for their families. At the end of the three-month period, they give back their precepts and return to family life.

All of these various precepts—those of the layman and laywoman and those of the various levels of monks and nuns—are included in what is broadly known as the *pratimoksha*, or precepts for individual liberation. The basic motivation we must cultivate to take these is the determination to be free from cyclic existence. These precepts regulate our actions of body and speech and are common to all the Buddhist traditions. No distinction among Theravada, Mahayana, or Vajrayana is made for the ordinations for individual liberation.

In the Mahayana tradition, there's a tradition of taking the eight precepts after strongly generating an altruistic motivation. When we take the precepts in this way, they are called "the eight Mahayana precepts." While monastics don't take the ordinary eight precepts for one day because they're included in their monks' and nuns' ordinations, they may take the eight Mahayana precepts.

Bodhisattva Precepts

On the basis of refuge or any of the ordinations for individual liberation, we may then take the bodhisattva ordination. This is done not only with the determination to be free from cyclic existence but also with the motivation of attaining enlightenment in order to benefit all beings. The bodhisattva vows focus on subduing the selfish attitude. They deal not only with our physical and verbal actions but also with our thoughts and attitudes. Thus, they're more difficult to keep than the vows for individual liberation.

The bodhisattva ordination is found only in the Mahayana traditions. It may be taken by laypeople or monastics. Although the essence is the same, the enumeration of the precepts varies in the Tibetan and the Chinese versions. When taking these precepts, we determine to keep them until attaining enlightenment, although they certainly need to be renewed each lifetime!

The Chinese have the custom of burning incense on the heads of monastics or on the arms of lay followers the evening before they take the bodhisattva precepts. This custom is unique to the Chinese and is not done by the other Buddhist traditions. It's done by placing three small pieces of incense on the head or on the arm, lighting them and allowing them to burn into the skin. Some people may choose to have more than three pieces of incense. There's no difference in status between those with more or less.

Although this ritual may sound gruesome to some people, it isn't that painful. Perhaps this is because the temple is resonating with the chanting of the Buddha's name and people aren't concentrating on their own pain.

The significance of this ritual is threefold. First, since the bodhisattva vows are taken with the motivation to attain enlightenment to benefit others, we must cultivate the courage to undergo suffering in the course of helping others. This isn't masochism, for we don't look for suffering. Rather, if we encounter bad circumstances in the process of working for others, we must be able to endure them. Enduring the pain of the incense burning into the skin signifies our courage and determination to help others no matter the cost to ourselves.

The second reason is to offer our bodies to the Buddha. Generally, we're very attached to and protective of our bodies. Here, that attachment is symbolically terminated by accepting some pain and thinking we offer our bodies to the Buddha.

The third reason is a practical one. In ancient China, monastics weren't subject to civil law as they were governed by the precepts and other monastic rules. However, neither the government nor the monasteries wanted common criminals to don the robes of ordained ones to escape punishment by civil law. Thus, this custom of burning incense on the monastics' heads was instituted in China to demarcate the ordained from the unordained.

Tantric Precepts

The third set of vows is the tantric precepts. Like the bodhisattva vows, these make us mindful of actions of body, speech, and mind. They focus chiefly on subduing the subtle dualistic view and the appearance and conception of things being ordinary, which are the final obstacles to the attainment of enlightenment. The tantric vows are the most difficult to keep purely. However, the benefit we receive from maintaining them is also greater.

Tantric vows are taken during some tantric initiations, and thus are found only in the Vajrayana tradition, which is a branch of the Mahayana. To take them, we must have taken refuge, some or all of the vows for individual liberation, and the bodhisattva vows. We pledge to keep the tantric vows until we attain enlightenment.

Taking Precepts

Taking any of the three sets of vows is entirely voluntary. To take them, we must understand the advantages of living ethically. There are innumerable benefits, but they may be abbreviated by saying that living in precepts leads us to liberation and enlightenment and enables us to make our lives useful for others.

Some people hesitate to take precepts because they feel they can't keep them purely. But we shouldn't expect ourselves to be perfect from the outset. If we could protect our precepts without one blemish, we wouldn't need to take them for we'd already be an arhat or a Buddha. Precepts are taken because we can't keep them perfectly. However, because they make us more aware of what we are doing, saying, thinking, and feeling, our actions, speech, and attitudes will improve.

Still we shouldn't take precepts if we're completely incapable of maintaining them. That would be foolish! We need a balanced attitude. It's like a child wanting to eat a piece of fruit. If she doesn't eat it because she's afraid it's too big, she'll miss out on something good. If she tries to put it in her mouth all at one time, she'll choke. By taking the amount that she can fit in her mouth, she'll grow. Similarly, we take precepts according to our ability to practice them.

To keep our precepts, we need to be very conscientious and mindful. If we transgress them, we can employ the four opponent powers—regret, refuge and the altruistic intention, remedial action, and the determination not to repeat the negative action—to purify the imprints left on our mindstreams. These four were described in Chapter 3 above, during the discussion of karma.

Precepts are regarded as the ornaments of a sincere practitioner. Even if we don't wish to take precepts, the effect of abandoning the ten destructive actions is immediately felt in our lives. The people around us notice the difference in our behavior and come to trust and respect us more. Our minds are calmer, and we can concentrate when we meditate. Ethical conduct is indeed the foundation of all temporal and ultimate happiness. As the Buddha said:

Sandalwood, tagara, lotus, and jasmine:
Above all these fragrances
The perfume of virtue
Is by far the best.

II   Our Relationships with Others

Each of us wonders, "How can I have a happy life? What will help me get along better with other people? How can I solve the problems that arise at work, at school, and at home?"

Buddhism addresses these very immediate concerns. For this reason, many people consider the Buddha's teachings to be a practical psychology, a guide to living a happy life. Complex philosophy or rituals aren't necessary to do this: Merely having a clear perspective on our lives is helpful.

This section grew from a request made by young adults in a meditation class I taught. They sought guidelines for having productive and gratifying relationships with others. In the *Sigalovada Sutra*, the Buddha gave practical advice on the principal relationships we have in our lives. Parts of the following chapters are taken from that sutra, as well as from other sutras and commentaries.

1 SPIRITUAL MENTOR:
RELATING REALISTICALLY TO A SPIRITUAL GUIDE

Some people wonder if it's necessary to have a spiritual master. Can we teach ourselves and discover the path alone? Can't we learn from books? To learn worldly skills, for example, reading, carpentry, surgery, or even driving a car, we need to be taught. It's difficult to learn on our own, and it could even be dangerous. Imagine trying to teach ourselves to pilot a plane! If we depend upon teachers to learn ordinary skills, then certainly we'll need the guidance of qualified teachers for spiritual matters, which are more profound and which influence not only this life but many future lives as well.

A living teacher can do what a book cannot do: answer our questions, act as an example of how to practice the teachings in daily life, encourage and inspire us on the path, and correct our behavior. Books can enrich and expand what we learn from our teachers, but they can't replace the spiritual relationship we form with a few wise people on the path.

The Sanskrit term for teacher, spiritual master, and spiritual mentor—all of which are synonymous—is *guru*. This refers to someone who is "weighty in good qualities." The Tibetan term *lama* means "unsurpassable."

There isn't an examination to pass to become a teacher. Rather, when others request someone for teaching and guidance, that person becomes their mentor. Some people are commonly referred to as "lama" or "master." This is because they have many students. However, whether they become *our* teacher is up to us. Similarly, other people may not generally be known as "lama" or "teacher," but if we choose them as our teachers, then they become our spiritual mentors.

When we're first learning about Buddhism, we may not have a specific spiritual master. That's fine. We can learn from a variety of teachers and practice accordingly. People who have only a general interest in Buddhism probably won't select a master. However, after a while, people who are serious in their practice will feel the need to establish a teacher-student relationship with spiritual masters so they can receive closer guidance.

Choosing Our Spiritual Mentors

Because our spiritual mentors will have a great influence on us, it's important to choose them carefully. For example, we don't marry just any person. We first look at the other's qualities and weaknesses, see if our dispositions are similar, and check if we feel we can care for that person through thick and thin. Similarly, it's advisable to examine a person well before taking him or her as our spiritual mentor.

Nowadays, we're faced with a spiritual supermarket: there are many teachers from which to choose. Anyone can teach one philosophy or another, put on a good show, and win over followers. But sincere seekers aren't interested in charisma; they look for substance.

It may take time to find and identify our masters. To start, we can attend talks and learn from people without accepting them as our masters. This enables us to examine both their character and our ability to relate to them well. We can take our time in deciding whether to accept someone as our master: the great Indian sage Atisha examined the renowned master Serlingpa for twelve years before taking him as his spiritual mentor.

It's not advantageous to select people as our spiritual mentors simply because they have many titles, sit on high seats, or wear impressive robes or hats. We shouldn't look for pomp, fame, or charisma, but instead seek out teachers who have excellent spiritual attributes. Also, we shouldn't select someone just because he or she is our friend's teacher. We must choose ourselves, according to the teacher's qualities and our experience with him or her.

In the *Mahayanasutralamkara,* Maitreya outlined ten qualities of excellent masters. He advised us to look for people who have:

1. Pure ethical discipline. Our teachers set an example for us. Because we need to modify our unruly actions of body, speech, and mind, it's wise for us to choose teachers who have done so. They

will instruct us how to improve ourselves and will be good examples for us to follow.

2. Experience in meditative concentration.

3. Deep understanding of the teachings on wisdom. These first three qualities show that someone is well trained in the three higher trainings that lead to liberation—ethical discipline, concentration, and wisdom.

4. More knowledge and a deeper realization of the subject to be taught than we have.

5. Enthusiastic perseverance to teach and guide their students. If we choose a person who doesn't enjoy teaching or is reluctant to guide others, we won't be able to learn very much.

6. Extensive learning from competent teachers. We want to learn from those who know the scriptures well and will teach according to them. People who make up their own teachings or misunderstand the Buddha's teachings can't show us the path to enlightenment.

7. Correct conceptual understanding or direct meditative insight into emptiness.

8. Skill to articulate the Dharma clearly so we'll understand it correctly.

9. Motivation of loving-kindness and compassion. This is a very important point. We can't trust someone who teaches in order to receive offerings, respect, or a large following. There is a danger that we'll be led astray by such a person, thereby wasting our lives and potentially engaging in negative activities. Therefore, it's extremely important to select as our masters people who have a pure and genuine wish to benefit their students and lead them on the path to enlightenment.

10. Patience and willingness to teach people of all levels of intelligence. We aren't perfect and will make mistakes due to our afflictions of anger and attachment. We need teachers who won't abandon us but will instead be patient and forgive us. In addition, we want teachers who won't be discouraged when we don't understand what they teach.

It may be difficult to find teachers with all of these qualities. In that case, the most important attributes they should have are:

1. They have more good qualities than faults.
2. They regard creating the ethical causes for happiness in future lives more important than enjoying the pleasures of this life.
3. They cherish others more than themselves.

Note that clairvoyance isn't mentioned as one of the qualities to look for in a master. There is a reason for this. Some people have clairvoyant powers but don't have knowledge of the path to enlightenment. Their clairvoyant powers are due to their previous karma, not to their Dharma practice, and thus they may not use their powers for altruistic purposes. Therefore, in seeking teachers to lead us on the path to enlightenment, it's wise to look for the qualities that Maitreya mentioned.

To learn what qualities teachers have, we can examine their behavior, their understanding of Dharma, and how they treat their students. It's not wise to ask Dharma teachers, "Are you enlightened?" for even if they were, they wouldn't tell us. The Buddha forbade his disciples to declare publicly what attainments they have. He wanted his followers to be humble, sincere, and unpretentious. Worldly people love to brag about their accomplishments; spiritual people are not like this. Their goal is to subdue the ego, not to enhance it.

We choose our spiritual mentors. When we decide that we would like someone to be our master, we can ask him or her personally to accept us as students. However, this isn't necessary; some masters are very busy with many students, so it's difficult to see them privately. In this case, we can make a strong mental decision that someone is our spiritual master. After that, when we again hear teachings from that person, he or she becomes our teacher. Also, if we take refuge, precepts, or empowerment (initiation) from someone, he or she automatically becomes our spiritual mentor.

We may have several spiritual masters, yet one remains the most important to us and is the one to whom we refer all serious matters. This master is called our "root spiritual master." This person is the one either who first made the Dharma touch our hearts and firmly set us on the path or with whom we feel the closest connection.

Following Our Mentors' Instructions, But Not Blindly

Having chosen a person as our spiritual mentor, we then follow that person's Dharma instructions to the best of our ability. In that way, we'll progress on the path.

Some people are fickle in their relationships with their masters and run from one master to another until they find one who tells them what they want to hear. Such students make little progress because of their own lack of commitment and respect.

We should care for our teachers, offering both our service and the requisites they need to live. When we appreciate the kindness of our teachers in showing us the path to happiness, we'll happily want to help them. As our teachers are working for the benefit of others and for the spread of the Dharma, our offerings will be put to good use.

Our Dharma practice is the best offering to make to our teachers. If we have material possessions, talents, and time, we can offer those. However, we don't neglect our practice, for that is what our teacher cares about most. When we follow the Dharma instructions we've received and keep whatever precepts we've taken, that pleases our teacher more than anything else.

When we notice what appear to be faults in our masters, it's counterproductive to criticize them angrily. Often we see faults in others simply because we're projecting onto their actions the motivation we would have if we acted like that. However, that may not be our teacher's motivation; he may do things for completely different reasons than we've supposed. In fact, our master may behave in a certain way to show us what we look like when we act like that.

It's easy for us to find faults in anyone and everyone, but doing so isn't advantageous if we're spiritual practitioners striving to develop tolerance and love. If we angrily criticize and reject our masters, we close the door to benefiting from all of their good qualities. That is a great loss.

However, if our master does something that seems contrary to the Buddha's teachings, we can ask him or her to explain that action. Alternatively, we can simply keep a respectful distance, not take that behavior as an example of how we should act, and cultivate relationships with other teachers whose behavior corresponds to the Buddha's teachings.

We relate to spiritual teachers to increase our wisdom and self-responsibility. Blindly following someone because "that person is my master so whatever he does is perfect" isn't acting intelligently. If our spiritual master asks us to do something that we're not able to do or that we feel isn't correct, we can respectfully tell him or her that we're unable to do that.

Being Honest

Our spiritual mentors are our best friends, and it's to our advantage to speak and act honestly with them. Some students are two-faced: they act well in the presence of their teachers, but at other times they gossip, lose their temper, and mistreat others. This is counterproductive.

Nor should we try to win our teacher's favor by pretentious sweet talk. Who are we fooling? Our master cares about the state of our minds, not about superficial appearances.

It's hypocritical to be kind to our teachers and rude to others. Our teachers want all beings to be happy, and thus we contradict our teachers' advice when we're belligerent and mean to others. If we hold our teachers in high esteem and other beings in contempt, we haven't understood the true meaning of the Dharma. To progress on the path, we need to treat both our teachers and other people with respect.

Let's think deeply about the meaning of respect. Some people confuse respect with fear and are then painfully shy and afraid of doing something wrong near a religious practitioner. There's no need to be emotionally immobilized like this. Interestingly, it may be our selfish mind that is afraid to look bad or foolish in front of someone else.

On the other hand, we shouldn't treat our masters like casual friends. A balance is required: Let's endeavor to have a good motivation and act well both when we're around our mentors and when we're not. But at the same time, let's not be afraid to admit our bad qualities to them. We can be honest with our teachers and seek their advice on how to improve.

Cherishing Our Teachers vs. Being Attached to Them

Some people confuse commitment to their teachers with attachment to them. This can be very painful, for if our teachers don't give us as much attention as we want, we then feel rejected. Attachment causes us to cling to our masters for emotional security, praise, and attention. But as we develop true appreciation of our teachers, we'll recognize their qualities and will be grateful for their kindness.

Attachment is self-oriented, while cherishing our teachers is based on sincere spiritual aspirations. Of course, we may miss our teachers when we're separated from them for a long time, but we must ask ourselves if we're missing them because we want Dharma teachings and guidance or because we want to feel loved.

The purpose of having a Dharma teacher isn't to please our egos but to destroy our ignorance and selfishness by practicing the teachings. Our teacher's job is not to meet our emotional needs but to lead us on the path to enlightenment. When our teachers point out our faults, we can be happy that they care for us enough to do this. They trust we'll welcome their advice rather than be offended. One time I saw a master tell a student his mistakes at a large gathering. I thought, "That must be a close disciple. The master knows that person wants to eliminate his egotistical pride and won't mind being publicly reprimanded." In fact, when I got to know the disciple, I discovered he was indeed a good practitioner.

Our relationships with our teachers will grow and develop over time. They can be very rewarding relationships, because by depending on wise and compassionate spiritual guides, we'll enhance our good qualities and eliminate our unwholesome ones. The closeness we feel with our spiritual mentors, who are genuinely concerned with our welfare and progress, is unlike the relationships we have with others. Our teachers will never stop helping us, no matter what we do. While this isn't a license for us to act recklessly, we needn't feel insecure that our teachers will cut off the relationship when we make mistakes. Our spiritual mentors are forgiving and compassionate, and we can therefore trust them.

As our understanding of the path to enlightenment deepens, so will our feeling of closeness with our teachers. This occurs because our minds become more similar to theirs. As our determination to be free increases and our altruistic motivation develops, we'll feel naturally close with our teachers, for we'll have the same interests and goals. Developing the wisdom realizing emptiness diminishes the feeling of separation that is caused by grasping at inherent existence. Eventually, when we become Buddhas, our realizations will be the same as those of our teachers.

2 PARENT AND CHILD:
BEING CLOSE WHILE LETTING GO

The relationship between parent and child is a unique and precious one, for it's due to the kindness of our parents that we're alive today. This is one of the most changeable of our relationships because it lasts over a long period of time, during which both parents and child as individuals go through many stages in life. Thus, both have to be sensitive to the changes occurring in the other, and to allow and support them.

With the easy availability of birth control, couples can now plan their families. It's wise to wait to have children when the marriage is stable and there is no financial difficulty in supporting children. However, if a child comes when it isn't expected, welcome it, for this being now has the opportunity to enjoy a human life.

The Buddha told Sigalo:

Householder, in these five ways parents discharge their responsibilities toward their children:
1. They restrain them from negative actions.
2. They establish them in virtuous actions.
3. They educate them in the arts and sciences.
4. They provide them with suitable wives and husbands.
5. They give them their inheritance at the proper time.

Parents do their best to restrain their children from actions that harm either themselves or others. They encourage their children to share what they have with others and to have a kind attitude toward others. If children are brought up to value ethical discipline and kindness, they'll become happy adults who will get along well with others. If children aren't taught how to be kind and happy people, then even if they have many academic degrees, their lives will be filled with difficulties.

Parents need to be good examples for their children. The old slogan of "Do what I say, not what I do" is a limp excuse for parents doing what they advise their children not to do. Children copy their parents' actions, and by acting hypocritically, parents are telling their children that hypocrisy and lying are acceptable. Thus, parents who want to help their children will live ethically and will be kind toward others.

Also, to help their children develop good characters, parents must spend time with them. Although both parents may work to support the home, becoming "workaholics" is not advisable. Working overtime to earn more money may seem appealing, but if that extra money has to be used to pay for the children to get counseling because they feel unloved, what use is it? Similarly, if the parents overwork and are stressed, the extra money is used to buy tranquilizers, pay for medical bills due to ulcers and heart attacks, or take vacations without the kids so they can relax. Overwork is self-defeating for the parents.

In addition, the children miss out on love and affection from their parents. Even if parents pay for music and art lessons and sports activities for their children, if the children feel unloved, all their lessons won't enable them to grow up to be happy adults. Western societies are witnessing tremendous increases in crime, drugs, divorce, and delinquent children. A lot of this is due to the breakdown of the family structure and the fact that parents don't spend enough quality time with their children. I hope modernizing Asian societies will learn from and avoid the mistakes of Western societies. Grasping for money at the expense of family closeness brings problems.

Parents give their children the best education they can and gear that education toward the child's disposition. If a child doesn't have musical ability, why torture him with forced music lessons? On the other hand, if a child has talent and interest in geology, the parents can encourage that.

In our modern world children are pressured from a young age to learn a lot and to be the best. This creates many psychological problems, for children need time to just be children and have fun. They need to be able to try new activities without being evaluated by tests and without their performance being compared to others. They need to be loved simply for who they are, without feeling they have to be the best.

Clearly, in our present Western society, parents don't arrange their children's marriages as in ancient India. Also, in those days, the family business—the inheritance—was passed on to the children when they were capable of running it, whereas today that isn't necessarily the case. However, I believe that the Buddha's fifth advice could mean that in today's society parents provide for the material well-being of their children as best as they can.

Parents care for their child's physical and material needs in a practical way. Obviously, they can't give more than their income allows. Giving children everything they want doesn't benefit them and may make them into nagging brats rather than kind people and good citizens. Parents must teach children how to deal with frustration because the inability of getting what we want is a situation all of us encounter numerous times in life. When children have unfulfilled wishes, explain that what they want is too expensive or isn't available. Help them understand that even if they had it, they wouldn't be completely happy and that by making a fuss, they are making themselves more unhappy. Explain to them the benefits of sharing possessions with others.

By helping their children deal with unfulfilled wishes, parents show them how to diminish their attachment, prevent them from taking things for granted, and help them to consider others' needs and wishes. Children often understand more than adults give them credit for. When something is explained calmly, logically, and repeatedly, in various circumstances that illustrate the point, children will understand.

Children will appreciate the possessions they have if they visit underdeveloped countries or impoverished areas in their own country. Seeing these places is an excellent education for them. In addition, parents can help their children make a habit of giving to charities in order to help those in need. By encouraging their children to think of others' welfare and to take joy in giving, parents free their children from the pain of self-absorption.

Children develop their self-images depending upon what the adults around them say. If children are often told they're naughty or stupid, they'll develop that self-concept and then will become like that. Thus, it's important to praise children and acknowledge what they do.

When correcting children's mistakes, parents should help them understand why that action was harmful. Also, it's important that children learn that although they made a mistake, it doesn't mean that they're bad people. If children start thinking that they—not the action they did—are bad, then that negative self-image will mold who they become.

Sometimes, in order to convey an important point to a child, parents may have to speak forcefully, but their minds can be imbued with compassion, not anger. In that way, they let the child know a certain action is not to be repeated, but they aren't angry and don't reject the child because he or she did it.

Being a parent means walking the fine line between the extremes of overprotecting one's children and neglecting them by not providing sufficient guidance. To counteract excess attachment and possessiveness, parents must remember that their children aren't their possessions. Children are unique personalities, who must learn to form their own opinions and make their own decisions.

By being too attached to a child, parents create the circumstance for their own unhappiness, for it's impossible for the child always to be with them. When their children grow up, some parents have difficulty in allowing their children to become more independent, for it means that they can't control their children's actions as closely and must trust the children's ability to make good decisions.

Some parents consistently tell their children what to do and what not to do. There is no discussion involved, for the children are expected simply to do what they're told. There are some situations where this is appropriate—for example, when a child's well-being is endangered and he lacks the ability to decide properly.

However, constantly telling children what to do doesn't help them to develop good judgment. Nor does it allow them to seek their parents' advice and discuss their problems with their parents. Children feel much closer to their parents if their parents listen and respond to them. When parents explain *why* a certain behavior is harmful or beneficial, it helps children to make wise decisions later. In this way, children learn to think clearly and act beneficially. Having trained their children to do this, parents then will feel more comfortable trusting their children. This helps to avoid the power struggle that so often happens during the teenage years.

Parents can't make their child conform to their image of a perfect child. Each child has his or her own potentials, and these may or may not correspond with what the parents want him or her to be. Parents can't expect their child to live their own unfulfilled dreams. While guiding their child to choose careers, spouses, and hobbies, parents must be mindful to have the child's interests, not their own, in mind. Wise parents accept their children as they are, while simultaneously guiding them to develop according to their capacities.

The other extreme is neglecting the child, which unfortunately happens too often in busy societies. Sometimes, in order to provide for the children's material well-being, the parents are too busy working to spend time with them or to give the love and guidance that they need. Parents need to allocate their time appropriately. It may be better to work less but have a more united family.

Parenting is a challenge and can enrich one's Dharma practice. The teachings on impermanence are apparent as children grow up. The disadvantages of anger and the importance of developing patience become clear when parents lose their temper in frustration at a child they want to help. An inkling of what it would be like to cherish all beings comes when parents think of loving everyone as much as they do their children. With mindfulness, parents and children can grow at the same time.

Understanding Our Parents

The topic of children's responsibilities toward their parents is a sensitive one nowadays. In societies where the family structure is breaking down, some children neglect to help their parents. Sometimes, because parents have continuously sought to fulfill the wishes and needs of their children, the children take this kindness for granted and expect their parents to provide everything for them. When children have this attitude, it not only hurts the parents but also leaves the children feeling disconnected and alone.

Many movements in psychology trace our insecurities and personality characteristics back to events that happened in childhood. Some people misinterpret this and blame their parents for all of their problems. Although it's important to understand the influence our upbringing had on us, we're adopting a victim mentality by considering our parents to be the source of our problems. Clinging to the past by thinking, "They did this and that, therefore, I have problems now," doesn't allow us to grow. We must assume responsibility for our own present insecurities and weaknesses and act to correct them.

Some children do grow up in dysfunctional families with negligent or abusive parents. It's important for these children to seek outside help so that they don't blame themselves for their parents' problems. However, they should avoid going to the other extreme and blame their parents for their own problems. Blame doesn't help heal emotional wounds. Understanding and forgiveness do.

In general, we're expert in enumerating others' faults and weak when it comes to remembering their good qualities and kindness. It's all too easy to blame our parents for their shortcomings and the consequent effects these had on us. Our parents may have done things while we were young that affected us negatively, but in their minds, they were doing the best they could given their own internal state of mind and the external circumstances. Thinking like this, we'll understand and forgive our parents, thus relieving the pain that anger and resentment cause.

If we complain that our parents don't understand and accept us for who we are, we also must ask whether we understand and accept our parents for who they are. It's hard to accept that our parents have faults and problems and that we can't make them become the ideal parents we envision. But when we can accept this, we'll be happier.

Children benefit themselves and their parents when they remember their parents' kindness. Our parents gave us this body and took care of us when we were helpless infants. They taught us to speak, gave us an education, and provided for us materially. Without their loving care, we would have starved during infancy or accidentally gotten hurt. As children, we didn't enjoy being disciplined when we misbehaved, but if our parents had not done so, we would have grown up to be rude and inconsiderate adults.

Teenagers often have difficulty getting along with their parents. They view themselves as adults and balk when their parents sometimes treat them as children. To most parents, however, teenagers are still children, and parents want to protect them. In fact, even when we're sixty years old, our parents will still see us as children. I chuckled when my grandmother told my father (who was sixty-five at the time) to put on a jacket so he wouldn't catch cold! If we accept this situation and are patient with our parents, our relationship will be smoother.

Also, it helps if teenagers recognize that their behavior isn't always consistent. Sometimes they want their parents to do many things for them, as if they were children who couldn't take care of themselves. Other times, they want their parents to treat them like self-sufficient adults. No wonder parents are confused! The best way for teenagers to demonstrate to their parents that they're mature is by being kind, helpful, and responsible.

Some parents have difficulty adjusting as their children grow up and become more independent. Parents may feel useless and unloved. As a result, some parents get depressed, while others become domineering or interfere with their children's lives. Rather than becoming belligerent at their parents' behavior, children can try to understand and address their parents' feelings. We can be sensitive to our parents' emotional needs and reassure them of our love, even though we're more independent.

Sometimes parents see potential dangers that we don't see; sometimes they have a long-range view while we only look at the momentary situation. In these cases, their advice is wise. Although their advice may seem to stifle our desires, often we can understand its value. We don't need to feel that our independence is compromised by following their advice. Rather, we can see its wisdom and thus voluntarily follow it.

If we feel that our parents are being unreasonable, we can try to discuss the situation with them. But first, it's beneficial for us to calm our anger. If we approach our parents with belligerence, we make it difficult for them to listen to us. Do we listen to people who are rude to us?

Even if our parents are unreasonable, they mean well. They're trying to help us and guide us as well as they can. For all of their faults, they mostly have good motivations. They may be short-sighted or concerned with things that we consider unimportant, but whatever their limitations are, they mean well. If we remember that, we'll recognize their love for us and won't get angry. We can feel grateful for their concern and then present our viewpoint to them, explaining it in a way that they can understand.

Our parents are conditioned and limited by their own preconceptions and upbringing. They grew up in a different social environment than we did, so they naturally see things differently. From their viewpoint, having grown up the way they did, most of what they think makes sense; just as growing up as we have, our perspective seems right to us.

If we only think of our parents' weaknesses, then they appear to us as full of faults. Thinking that way makes us ignore the good qualities they have. If we remember their kindness and the care they have shown us, we'll see their good qualities and our hearts will open with love. We won't be stubborn and rude, so our parents will listen more to what we have to say.

The Buddha told Sigalo five ways for children to fulfill their responsibilities to their parents:

1. They support and protect their parents and supply their wants.
2. They perform the duties their parents delegate to them.
3. They maintain the good name of the family.
4. They conduct themselves in such a way as to deserve the inheritance of parental property.
5. They give alms in the name of their parents when they are dead, and dedicate the positive potential to them.

It's only fair that children do their share of household chores and work for the benefit of the entire family. And, since parents cared for and supported the children while they were young and helpless, children should happily reciprocate when their parents are sick or aged. If the children can't care for their parents themselves, they can ensure that someone else does.

Some elderly people are demanding, but if we consider how life appears to them, we'll be more tolerant of the difficulties they have growing old. If we think about how we would feel being them, we'll be more understanding. When we're old, we certainly will want our children to care for us.

To repay the kindness of their parents, children try to live according to the good ethical values their parents taught them. They conduct themselves well, causing their parents less worry and also preventing them from being criticized or ashamed. In this way, too, children make themselves worthy of receiving inheritance from their parents.

After the parents' death, children can make offerings and prayers and dedicate the positive potential accumulated by these for their parents' happiness and good rebirth. Of course, if we really want to benefit our family members, it's best to encourage them while they're alive to act constructively and avoid harmful actions. We can act in all the ways mentioned above to have a good relationship with our parents.

3 FRIENDSHIP:
SHARING AND CARING

In the *Dhammapada*, the Buddha said:

> Just as the clean kusha grass
> That wraps a rotten fish
> Will also start to rot,
> So too will those devoted to an unwholesome person.

> Just as a leaf folded
> To contain an incense offering
> Also becomes sweet,
> So too will those devoted to the virtuous.

Our friends influence us a lot. Thus, our choice of friends affects the kind of people we'll become. We can see how much our companions influence us by looking at our own experiences: think of times when we were unhappy or in trouble and notice how much those situations were due to being with the wrong people. Similarly, think of the happiness we've had and knowledge we've gained through being in the company of caring friends.

What qualities make people good friends? Which are better to avoid? For the sake of brevity, I've paraphrased the section in the *Sigalovada Sutra* about friendship. Reflecting on each point and thinking of examples from our lives will help us gain clarity about our friendships.

Although the points are expressed in terms of the qualities we want to look for in others, it's equally important for us to check if we have those qualities ourselves. The following points are very practical advice on which personality traits to discourage and which to develop in ourselves so that others will be attracted to us and we'll be good friends to others.

There are four kinds of false friends, who are actually foes in the disguise of friends:

1.   Those who come empty-handed but leave with something. These are people who:
   • visit us with the intention of taking our things
   • give us a little but expect to receive a lot in return
   • help us only when they're in danger
   • associate with us only out of selfish motives

2.   Those who pay us lip service and whose friendship is only skin-deep. These are people who:
   • entertain us and waste our time by talking of the past
   • entertain us and waste our time by talking of the future
   • try to gain our favor by offering help when help isn't needed
   • when we ask for help, give excuses and don't help

3.   Those who flatter us, seeming to care for us when they actually don't. These are people who:
   • encourage us to act negatively
   • discourage us from acting positively
   • praise us in our presence
   • criticize us behind our backs

4.   Those who lead to our ruin. These are people who:
   • are our companions in drinking or taking drugs
   • roam the streets with us when it's late
   • accompany us to see unwholesome entertainment
   • go gambling with us

Having an open and trusting relationship with people like these is difficult. It's better to keep them at a distance, but without criticizing them. Although we can say some behavior isn't good, we can't say the people who do it are evil, irredeemable people. We can still have compassion for them and wish them well, but we don't seek their company, for we know it will lead us in a direction we don't want to go.

Similarly, the Buddha described the qualities of good friends. These are people we can trust and on whom we can rely. By associating with them, we'll be happy and our characters will improve. As well as seeking the company of people with good qualities, it's important to develop these traits within ourselves.

The four kinds of good-hearted friends are:

1. Those who help us. These are people who:
    - guard us when we're careless or not paying attention
    - protect our possessions
    - help and console us in times of fear
    - give more than asked for when we request their help

2. Those who care for us in good times and bad. These are people who:
    - confide in us
    - keep what we tell them confidential
    - don't forsake us when we're troubled or face calamity
    - would even sacrifice their lives for us

3. Those who encourage us in a positive direction and cause us to become better people. These are people who:
    - dissuade us from doing negative actions
    - persuade us to do positive actions
    - cause us to listen to beneficial teachings
    - indicate to us the path to happiness

4. Those who are compassionate and sympathetic. These are people who:
    - sympathize with us in times of adversity
    - rejoice at our prosperity and fortune without being jealous
    - dissuade others from speaking ill of us
    - praise those who speak well of us

Although what has been said above is very general, and we may feel we learned it when we were children, it's valuable to reflect on our relationships and actions to see how well we practice this advice now. By taking general principles and applying them to specific situations in our lives, we'll get to know ourselves better and will have a better idea of how we want to grow.

Love and Attachment

People often wonder how to reconcile the Buddha's teachings on non-attachment with those on love. How can we love others without being attached to them? Non-attachment is a balanced state of mind in which we cease overestimating others' qualities. By having a more accurate view of others, our unrealistic expectations fall away, as does our clinging. This leaves us open to loving others for who they are, instead of for what they do for us. Our hearts can open to care for everyone impartially, wishing everyone to be happy simply because he or she is a living being. The feeling of warmth that was previously reserved for a select few can now be expanded to a great number of people.

With some people we share many common interests. It's easy to talk to them; we understand each other well and help each other grow. We may spend more time with these people than with others. They can be our friends without our clinging to them with attachment. The focus of such a friendship is mutual growth, not fulfillment of our selfish desires.

Since it's difficult to free ourselves from attachment, initially our friendships will be a combination of attachment and genuine love. But, being aware of the disadvantages of attachment, we'll try to eliminate it so it doesn't cause problems in our relationships. Slowly, the quality of our friendships will improve.

Helping Our Friends

It's important for us to be sensitive to others' needs and wishes. This involves having respect and appreciation for people as unique individuals. It also entails our not being self-centered and demanding. As soon as we start thinking more of our own benefit than of mutual benefit in a relationship, problems will arise.

Sometimes we have a "take take" mentality. We view everything and everyone in terms of what we can get from them. Neglecting to consider our effect on others, we think only of how others benefit or harm us. This attitude leads us to have problems with others, for no matter what others do or how kind they are, we're never satisfied. We become grouchy and discontent, making ourselves and those around us miserable.

The "take take" mentality shows itself very clearly when we enter a room full of strangers. Do we usually think as we walk in, "How can I benefit the people here? What are their needs? What pain are they experiencing that I can help to remove?" Usually, such an other-centered attitude is far from our minds, and instead we're engrossed wondering, "Who has connections that can help me? Will people ignore me or put me down? Will that good-looking person over there like me?"

It's interesting to pause a moment before going into a room and think, "In this life and in my previous lives, all beings have been kind to me. Now is my chance to return their kindness. No matter what they look like on the surface, these people are just like me: They sometimes feel insecure and want to be appreciated; they like to be acknowledged as worthwhile individuals. I'm going to use this time with them to give whatever I can." Our experience in interviews, at parties, and during meetings will be considerably different if we practice thinking like this.

Gradually, we'll develop a "give give" mentality, thinking of what we can do for others. When we have this attitude our own problems don't seem so enormous and we're happy whomever we're with. Others are happy, they like us, and inside our hearts, we're satisfied, for we know that our lives are meaningful.

Part of being sensitive to others involves knowing when to talk and what to say. Let's not waste others' time with our frivolous chatter. This is actually more difficult than it sounds, for we may think something is important and interesting, while others may not. Being aware of others' values and priorities will make us more considerate.

Being considerate and generous doesn't mean we suppress our own self-development in order to do whatever others want. There is a difference between being kind to others out of genuine affection for them and denying our own self-worth to do what others say just to gain their approval. Before we can have a kind heart, we have to have self-respect.

On the other hand, self-respect is different from selfishness. With the former we recognize our worth as human beings, with the latter we cling to our happiness as if it were more important than that of others. A balance point between self-abnegation and selfishness is to recognize the fundamental equality of ourselves and all others: We all seek happiness and wish to avoid problems. We all have good qualities and weaknesses. We're all worthy of respect simply because we're living beings.

Peer Pressure

Although we usually think of peer pressure occurring among young people, in fact, it influences us no matter what our age or with whom we associate. None of us enjoys being insulted or misunderstood, and we all want others to think well of us. Although we know that if certain people ridicule or criticize us, we shouldn't pay attention, still we don't like to hear what they say. Thus, we may join in their activities to receive their friendship and avoid their antagonism.

What is at issue is our self-confidence. When we rely on others' praises to feel worthwhile, we go up and down emotionally, depending on what others say. We become extremely vulnerable and are easily influenced because we don't know clearly what we believe, or even if we do know, we lack the confidence to express it.

It's important to contemplate deeply that someone telling us we're good doesn't make us good and someone criticizing us doesn't make us bad. Praise and blame are only others' impressions and opinions; they're not what we really are. We have to examine our own attitudes and behavior and develop a realistic view of ourselves. In that way, we can assess our own strengths and weaknesses.

If someone accurately points out our weaknesses or mistakes, there's nothing to be alarmed at. It's like someone saying, "There's a nose on your face." It's there for everyone to see, so trying to hide our mistakes is useless. Being offended when someone else notices what is obvious is equally as senseless. Let's just accept that we made a mistake and apologize.

If someone tells us we have horns on our head, we aren't insulted for it's clear the other person is mistaken. Similarly, if we're blamed for something that we didn't do, or if others exaggerate what we did, there's no need to be angry. What they're saying is simply incorrect.

We all have good qualities, and it's important to acknowledge them. However, there's no reason to be proud of our talents and achievements, for they came about due to the kindness of others. If others didn't teach us and help us, we wouldn't have been successful. In the same way as we can accept our mistakes without resentment, we can receive others' praise without conceit. The Buddha said:

As a solid rock is not shaken by the wind,
So too the wise remain unshaken amidst blame and praise.

The ability to be emotionally balanced whether others praise or blame us allows us to evaluate and learn from what they say. In this way, we gain a clearer picture of ourselves and thus will be less susceptible to negative peer pressure.

Another factor contributing to our self-confidence is a clear sense of ethical values. When we have this, we won't get confused in potentially harmful situations, nor will we fall prey to the misleading influence of others. If we think deeply about the advantages and disadvantages of certain actions, we'll reach clear conclusions about our ethical values. Even if someone then criticizes or ridicules us for not joining in their unwholesome activities, our minds won't move because we'll know that what we're doing is correct. Developing a deep sense of self-confidence and ethical values requires much thought on our part.

Discussing Problems

Sometimes we need to discuss our problems with friends. How can we do this in a beneficial manner, so that we don't burden them with our difficulties and negative feelings? Sometimes we may need to "let it all out," and a good friend is someone who will listen with an open and compassionate heart.

While it's fine to relate our difficulties to those close to us, it's not very beneficial to dump our emotional confusion onto them and leave it at that. Similarly, it's not productive to tell our problems to our friends merely to gain their sympathy and to have them agree how mean and unfair someone was to us. That only increases our self-pity and doesn't solve our problem!

Once we've acknowledged and accepted that we have a problem, negative feelings, or confusion, the next step is to work it out. One way is to seek honest and constructive feedback from our friends. We'll welcome their truthful assessments, even when they tell us that we were mistaken or that we brought on the problem ourselves. Friends who point out when we exaggerate the situation or when we are inflexible help us. Instead of telling us we're right even when we're not, our friends will assist us in identifying and solving our problems.

Knowing the value of good friendships, we'll seek the company of those who influence us positively. In addition, we'll try to diminish our faults and increase our good qualities so we can become better friends to others.

4 COLLEAGUES AND CLIENTS:
WORKING TOGETHER AND RESOLVING DIFFERENCES

We can develop the lofty goal of becoming Buddhas for the benefit of all beings while we're seated in meditation. But we must also be down-to-earth and practice love and compassion toward those around us, especially the people with whom we work. Living ethically, appreciating others' efforts, and resolving differences are ways to do this.

Living Ethically

Ethical discipline forms the basis for living together peacefully and prosperously. People who are trustworthy in their jobs not only win the respect of their bosses, colleagues, and clients, but their careers are also more successful in the long run. If we charge fair prices, render good service, and are honest with clients, they'll continue to do business with us and will refer others to us as well.

On the other hand, neglecting ethical discipline by doing whatever fulfills our selfish momentary purposes brings disharmony and eventually harms our career. In recent years, several prominent people in business and government have been convicted of violating the law and were publicly disgraced. Their greed for money and prestige was the source of their dishonesty and eventual downfall.

People hesitate to do business with those who are known to be ruthless. If we lie or are dishonest with our bosses, colleagues, or clients, we'll lose their respect and cooperation. Although we may temporarily benefit from selfish ways of conducting business, in the long run we'll be unable to work well with others during the day or to sleep with a clear conscience at night. Abandoning the ten destructive actions will prevent these difficulties.

Appreciating Others

Helping our colleagues and appreciating their work makes them happy and builds a spirit of teamwork. When others feel their efforts have been recognized, they're more cooperative and work harder. If they are given avenues to air their opinions, they feel more involved and loyal to their company.

But our motivation in praising others mustn't be just to increase their productivity! Insincerity is quickly uncovered and it spoils working relations. Respecting and appreciating others—including those "inferior" to us in terms of position, education, and so forth—is a key element in our development of love and compassion. Therefore, we must remember that a boss can't be successful without the work of her staff, a company can't function without its employees. Our success, therefore, isn't our own; it's due to the kind efforts and cooperation of others. Thus, listening to, respecting, and praising them is suitable.

Staff and workers, too, need to recognize the efforts of their bosses. It's easy to complain and criticize and difficult to acknowledge that others do their best, even though they aren't perfect. Although workers should give constructive feedback on unfair company policies, gossiping behind others' backs and fomenting disharmony only create more problems for everyone.

Resolving Difficulties

As long as we're in cyclic existence, we'll have problems and conflicts with others. They challenge us to be creative in how we communicate and solve our problems. What are ways to do this? First, the Buddha advised:

> Do not look out for others' flaws,
> For what they do or do not do,
> But look out for what one oneself
> Should do and should not do.

Being aware of and responsible for our own attitudes and actions is more effective in having good relations than telling others what they should do.

Numerous are the examples of problems arising because we focus more on criticizing others' behavior and gossiping about them than on what we do. It's easy to point out others' faults, but we don't like to look at our own.

This attitude doesn't bring the results we desire. Although we may notice others' weaknesses, we can't correct them. Our own faults, which we have the power to remedy, can't be corrected if we ignore them. Although we can influence others' attitudes and actions, we can never control them, for each person is in charge of his or her own actions, words, and thoughts. Thus, demanding that others change is unrealistic. In any relationship, we can only dictate our own behavior, and even that isn't so easy to do!

When differences arise at work, we can approach the situation by first thinking how it appears through the eyes of the other person. This enables us to understand his or her position and feelings and thereby be understanding rather than angry. We may also discover that we accidentally (or even deliberately) did something to disturb the other person. We can then apologize.

Some people resist apologizing for fear of losing face. However, by refusing to admit their mistakes, they increase tension and bad feelings. In actual fact, people who are able to apologize are courageous. They speak not from a position of weakness but one of strength because they have the self-confidence and integrity to admit and remedy their mistakes. Only a cowardly person hides his errors and stubbornly refuses to admit them.

However, if upon investigation it seems we haven't erred, then we can talk directly with the other person to resolve the misunderstanding or disagreement. This can be done without anger, after having calmed our minds by applying the techniques the Buddha taught for subduing anger. Then we can express the problem to our colleague, without accusing or blaming him, for that only worsens the situation by putting him on the defensive. Rather, we can say, for example, "When you act like this, I feel upset (or however we feel) because...," and explain why we feel this way. In this way, we're owning our feelings rather than blaming them on the other person. Also, we're explaining to our colleague the impact his actions have on us and why we feel the way we do. We can then add, "I'm not happy feeling like that. Please explain why you do this, so I can understand."

In such a way, we give the other person space to explain his viewpoint. When he responds, we try to listen and understand what he says, without interrupting. Sometimes this requires great patience on our part, for the temptation to interrupt and explain why he's wrong is great; but in the end, listening with an open mind allows dialogue to follow.

In situations of conflict, it's helpful to think of ourselves and the other person being side by side, approaching the problem together. Rather than envisioning the two parties as opponents in a battle that will have a winner and a loser, we can see the situation as a mutual problem needing mutual cooperation to resolve. In that way, we will collaborate to find a solution beneficial to both of us.

Sometimes we may be jealous of our colleagues. This painful emotion can be resolved by viewing our colleagues' success from a different perspective. If they have qualities, talents, or opportunities that we don't, we can rejoice at their happiness and good fortune. We aren't the only one who seeks happiness; others do as well. Besides, we often say, "Wouldn't it be wonderful if everyone were happy!" Now we must make our feeling consistent with our words. Our colleague is successful, and we didn't have to do anything to make her happy! This is cause for rejoicing, not for painful jealousy. By rejoicing at another's fortune, both of us are happy!

In this way, constructively relating to people at work becomes our Dharma practice. It challenges us to integrate the Buddha's teachings with our ways of thinking, so that the teachings aren't mere intellectual knowledge but become part of our personality. This not only enables us to progress along the path, but also makes our present relationships more harmonious.

5 MARRIAGE:
HELPING EACH OTHER GROW

All that has been said above regarding selecting friends and the manner in which friends treat each other applies equally to the relationship between boyfriend and girlfriend or husband and wife. Friendship and common interests are essential in order to form a firm foundation for a couple relationship. Rather than having a relationship based on sexual attraction or excess emotional dependency, a couple will have a more lasting and satisfying relationship if they're friends who trust, encourage, and are patient with each other.

It must be added that not all people wish to have a partner. This is an individual choice, depending on each person's character and on other factors. If some people choose to remain single, that could be the best way for them to be happy and productive. Marriage is not for everyone.

Pop music and films present us with an idealistic view of romantic relationships. If we take this as our example, we run into problems because we're searching for Mr. or Ms. Perfect. Attachment makes us project qualities onto another person or exaggerate the good qualities he or she has, and we get caught in a whirlwind of excitement and romance.

However, the bubble eventually pops. This happens not because we or the other person do something wrong, but because we have unrealistic expectations and don't give the other person the space to be him or herself. Or, we may have had dreams of a perfect relationship free from disagreement. These false expectations created by attachment only lead us to disappointment.

It's much better to be aware that the other person has both good qualities and weaknesses and that the relationship will have ups and downs. Sometimes two people will be very close and at other times they won't be as close. This is natural, and we should expect it.

It's impossible for another person to fulfill us completely. Why? Because he or she has limitations. In addition, our mind isn't constant. What we want and expect from another is subject to change.

Likewise it's impossible for another person to solve all of our problems and insecurities. Only we can solve our problems by practicing the appropriate antidotes to free ourselves from anger, attachment, confusion, jealousy, and pride. Understanding this, we'll have patience, mutual respect, and an ability to forgive, enabling the relationship to grow and continue.

When two people enter into a romantic relationship seeking self-satisfaction, each one considers his or her personal wishes and needs more important than the other's. This is the basis of all quarrels. This selfish attitude leads to a dead end, for each party refuses to relinquish his or her desires. Our job is to subdue our own self-centeredness, not to nag the other person to get rid of his or hers.

Marriage is an opportunity to practice cherishing others more than ourselves. A relationship will be stable and enduring if both people think the main purpose of being together is to help each other and to help others. If one person is upset or under the influence of a disturbing emotion, the other will encourage him or her to look at the situation from a different viewpoint. Or, if both people are in the habit of having quiet time alone to think, and one becomes distracted and neglects his or her quiet time, the other will gently encourage him or her to re-focus on personal and spiritual development. Such mutual support and encouragement strengthens their relationship.

Mutual respect is crucial in a marriage, and this is shown through how we speak and act toward the other. Slanderous or reproachful language doesn't lead to harmony. Neither does any type of physical violence. When we're angry, we make everyone miserable if we vent it on those near us. Being sarcastic or condescending, or teasing our partner about a sensitive issue doesn't bring happiness to either of us.

If we develop respect for both ourselves and our partner, we'll think before we speak because we'll care about the effect our words have on the other. We'll show our respect by caring for mutual possessions, as well as for our partner's personal belongings. If he or she has interests or engages in activities that we don't share, we won't mind, for we'll recognize that the other person isn't our personal property. He or she is a unique individual who wants to develop many sides of his or her personality.

Respect is equally necessary when relating to our partner's family. Whether or not we like our in-laws, it's important to speak and act toward them with consideration. That doesn't mean we let them run our lives, for they may have different priorities or a different life style from ours. However, we can still listen to others' advice and thank them for it, although we may or may not follow it. Being belligerent to our in-laws doesn't create harmony, while respecting them as human beings does. Being jealous of our partner's affection for his or her family also creates tension. It's much better if we respect their care for each other.

Trust is important and is built up by both people being caring and responsible in carrying out their commitments. With the change in gender-identified roles of men and women in our society, each couple needs to divide the duties of running a household and raising a family in a fair way, agreeable to both people. Each person then fulfills his or her responsibilities, thus increasing the trust between them.

Trust is also built up by being truthful to the other person. Thus, it's good to avoid doing things that we have to lie about. If we do make a mistake, let's apologize. On the other hand, if our partner apologizes to us, we can forgive him or her and try to let go of any hurt feelings or the wish for revenge. Forgiving someone does not mean we condone their action. Rather, we simply let go of our anger.

Fidelity is another way to maintain and increase trust in a marriage. If we're dissatisfied and desire another sexual partner, we must examine from where this attitude comes. Does it point to a problem in the relationship that we need to discuss and solve with our partner? Or are we merely itchy, bored, and fantasizing? In this case, we can remind ourselves that acting on this dissatisfaction will only cause confusion and pain for ourselves, our partner, our children, and the third person. It's important to remember the effects our actions have on others. By caring more about others' feelings and less about our own whims, we won't have extramarital sexual relationships.

Trust must also be cultivated in managing the family's money. Each couple should discuss and decide how to handle their money. Whatever is decided upon, we must take care to follow the agreement. Squandering the family's money for our own pleasure, gambling, or spending more than the budget can support impedes mutual trust and causes financial problems. For that reason, it's wise to consult the other person before making a major purchase, and if that person has strong reservations, to wait. If we respect our partner and cherish him or her, we'll use money neither as a tool of power over the other nor for our own selfish pleasure.

Whether we marry or not is our own personal decision. In Buddhism, marriage isn't a holy matter, and there's no obligation to marry in order to perform a religious duty. Since marriage is seen as a secular affair, there is no "Buddhist view" on same-sex marriages. The same values of mutual respect and care are important in all relationships.

Similarly, from a Buddhist perspective, there is no obligation that a couple have children. They may want to have more time for Dharma practice or social welfare projects, in which case they may agree not to have children. Other couples may feel that having a family is important. It's their personal decision whether or not to have children and how many to have.

When parents share a common view of how to raise the children, children don't get confused about what they may and may not do. Children need consistent guidance from both parents. If a parent is inconsistent in his or her actions toward the children, or if the parents teach or do things that contradict each other, the children become very confused. This also could lead to quarrels between the parents. Frequent discussion and good communication between parents will prevent or solve this difficulty.

It may happen that although two partners try to resolve their conflicts, they are unsuccessful and, after a while, feel that it's difficult to continue living together. Just as marriage is a secular matter in Buddhism, so are separation and divorce. There is no religious stigma against it. If either person wishes to remarry, he or she may.

However, Buddhism encourages cooperation and harmony among people, as well as patience and forgiveness when differences of opinion or detrimental actions occur. Married people should do their best to be aware of and be considerate of their spouse's feelings. Running from one person to another or from one situation to another in search of more and better happiness is a fruitless quest, which only breeds more dissatisfaction. Thus, whenever possible, it's better for a couple to work out their marital difficulties, especially for the sake of the children.

Regarding this, His Holiness the Dalai Lama counseled in *Kindness, Clarity, and Insight:*

> It is not sufficient that a couple think of only their own love affairs and their own pleasure. You have a moral responsibility to think of your children. If the parents divorce, the child is going to suffer, not just temporarily but for his or her whole life. The model for a person is one's own parents. If the parents are always fighting and finally divorce, I think that unconsciously, deep down, the child is badly influenced, imprinted. This is a tragedy. Thus, my advice is that for real marriage, there is no hurry: Proceed very cautiously, and marry only after good understanding; then you will have a happy marriage. Happiness in the home will lead to happiness in the world.

Thus, if people approach marriage with a realistic attitude, commitment, humility, patience, respect, and sincere care for the other person, they will learn and grow through the years. To possess these qualities, we need to reflect on our actions, modify any harmful thoughts or deeds, and cultivate our good qualities.

III   TAMING BAD HABITS, CULTIVATING GOOD ONES

We are very much creatures of habit. But that doesn't mean we simply sit back and live on automatic. Rather, we endeavor to tame our bad habits and to cultivate beneficial ones in their place. In this way our lives will become peaceful now, and we will create the causes for happiness in the future, including liberation and enlightenment. In addition, because we live interdependent with all other beings, those around us will benefit from the changes in us. This is our contribution to world peace.

1   COMPLAINING: A FAVORITE PASTIME

Some of us frequently find ourselves indulging in our "favorite" pastime: complaining. It's not exactly our favorite activity, because it makes us more miserable, but it's certainly one that we engage in often. We don't always see what we're doing as complaining; in fact, we often think we're simply telling the truth about the world. But when we look carefully, we are forced to acknowledge that our woebegone statements are actually complaints.

What constitutes complaining? One dictionary defines it as, "An expression of pain, dissatisfaction, or resentment." I would add that it's a statement of dislike, blame, or judgment that we whine about repeatedly.

Contents of Complaints

We complain about anything and everything. "My flight has been cancelled." "The insurance company refused to hear my claim." "It's too hot." "My friend is in a bad mood."

We complain about our wealth, or lack of it. No matter how much one possesses, no one ever feels that it is enough. We grumble that it's not fair that others have more money than we do and that they have better opportunities to earn it.

We complain about our health. This is not limited to the ill and elderly. "My back hurts." "My allergies are acting up." "I have a headache." "My cholesterol is too high." "I'm exhausted." "My heart beats irregularly." "My kidneys don't work right." "My little toe is infected." We can talk about our own aches and pains without tiring of the topic, although we find listening to others do the same boring.

One of the juiciest topics of complaint is others' actions and personalities. We resemble mental gossip columnists. "My colleague at work doesn't turn in his work on time." "My boss is too bossy." "My employees are ungrateful." "After everything I did for my kids, they moved to another town, and they don't come home for holidays." "I'm fifty, and my parents are still trying to run my life." "This person talks too loud."

Complaining about political leaders and the government—not just our own, but others' too—is a national pastime in the USA. We bemoan unfair policies, the brutality of oppressive regimes, the injustice of the justice system, and the cruelty of the global economy. We write e-mails to friends who have the same political views as we do and hope they will do something to change the situation.

In essence, we complain about whatever meets with our disapproval.

Why Do We Complain?

We complain for a variety of reasons. In all the cases, we're looking for something, even though we may not be aware of what it is at the time.

Sometimes we complain because we simply want someone to recognize our suffering. Once they do, something inside us feels satisfied, but until they do, we go on and on telling our story. For example, we may tell the story of a dear one betraying our trust. When our friends try to fix the problem, we feel more frustrated. We may even feel that they're not hearing us. But when they say, "You must be very disappointed," we feel heard—our misery has been acknowledged—and we say no more.

At other times, we continue to lament despite others' understanding. For example, we may repeatedly complain about our health out of self-pity or the wish to gain others' sympathy. Others may be sympathetic, but no matter what they say or do for us, we are dissatisfied.

We may complain in the hopes that someone will fix our problem. Instead of asking someone directly for help, we recount our sad story again and again in the hopes that someone will get the message and change the situation for us. We may do this because we're too lazy or frightened to try to solve the problem ourselves. For instance, we complain to a colleague about a disturbing situation at work in the hopes that she will go to the manager about it.

We complain to vent our emotions and our feelings of powerlessness. We criticize government policies, the corruption of CEOs, and the activities of politicians that prevent them from actually caring for the country. We dislike these things, but we feel powerless to change them, so we preside over what amounts to a court case—either mentally or with our friends—in which we prosecute, convict, and banish the people involved.

"Venting" is often used to justify ranting about whatever we want. One friend told me that he regularly hears people say, "I have to vent! I'm so angry, I just can't help it." Such people seem to feel that they will explode if they don't let off some steam. However, shouldn't we take into account the consequences, for ourselves and others, of venting? In the Buddha's teachings we find many other options to resolve our frustration and anger without spewing them out on others.

Discussing vs. Complaining

What is the difference between complaining and discussing certain topics in a constructive way? Here, our attitude or our motivation for speaking is chief. Discussing a situation involves taking a more balanced approach, in which we actively try to understand the origin of the problem and consider various possible remedies. We are proactive, not reactive. We assume responsibility for what is our responsibility and cease blaming others when we cannot control a situation.

Thus, it's possible to discuss our health without complaining about it. We simply tell others the facts and go on. If we need help, we ask for it directly, instead of lamenting in the hopes that someone will rescue us or feel sorry for us. Similarly, we can discuss our financial situation, a friendship gone awry, an unfair policy at work, the uncooperative attitude of a salesperson, the ills of society, the misconceptions of political leaders, or the dishonesty of CEOs without complaining about them. This is far more productive, because discussion with knowledgeable people can give us and them new perspectives on the situation, which, in turn, helps us deal with it more effectively.

Antidotes to Complaining

For Buddhist practitioners, several meditations act as healthy antidotes to the habit of complaining. Meditating on impermanence is a good start. Seeing that everything is transient enables us to set our priorities wisely and determine what is important in life. It becomes clear that the petty things about which we complain are not important in the long run, and we let them go.

Meditating on compassion is also helpful. When our mind is imbued with compassion, we don't view others as enemies or as obstacles to our happiness. Instead, we see that they do harmful actions because they wish to be happy but don't know the correct method for attaining happiness. They are, in fact, just like us: imperfect, limited sentient beings who want happiness and not suffering. Thus, we can accept them as they are and seek to benefit them in the future. We see that our own happiness, in comparison to the problematic situations others experience, is not so important. Therefore, we are able to view others with understanding and kindness, and any inclination to complain about, blame, or judge them evaporates.

Meditating on the nature of cyclic existence is another antidote. Seeing that we and others are under the influence of ignorance, anger, and clinging attachment, we abandon idealistic visions that things should be a certain way. As a friend says to me when I mindlessly complain, "This is cyclic existence. What do you expect?" I suppose that at that moment, I expected perfection, that is, that everything should happen the way I want it to. Examining the nature of cyclic existence frees us from such unrealistic thinking and from the complaining it foments.

In his *Guide to the Bodhisattva's Way of Life*, Shantideva counsels, "If something can be changed, work to change it. If it cannot, why worry, be upset, or complain?" Let's remember this wise advice when the urge arises to complain.

When Others Complain

What can we do when someone incessantly complains to us about something we cannot do anything to change? Depending on the situation, there are a few possibilities.

One is reflective listening. Taking someone's suffering seriously, we listen with a compassionate heart. We reflect back to the person the content or the feeling he or she expresses: "It sounds like the diagnosis frightened you." "You were relying on your son to take care of that, and he was so busy he forgot. That left you in the lurch." Feeling understood, the person is free to move on to other topics.

Another technique is to change the subject. I had an elderly relative who, whenever I visited, would complain about every member of the family. Needless to say, I was uninterested as well as dismayed to see him work himself into a bad mood. So, in the middle of a tale, referring to something he had said, I would lead the discussion in another direction. If he were complaining about someone's cooking, I would ask if he had seen the delicious-sounding recipes in the Sunday paper. We would begin to talk about the paper, and he would forget his previous complaints and turn to more satisfying topics of discussion.

Joking with the person may also help. Let's say someone is melodramatic about her ailments, draws others into her predicaments, and tries to turn all attention to her own suffering. Avoiding her may not always be possible, and telling her she has nothing to complain about only aggravates the situation. But if we can earnestly smile and be playful, she may relax. For example, in an exaggerated manner so the person knows we are joking, we could pretend to be ill and seek her help. Or we could respond to her melodrama by being pretending to rescue her in a playful way that makes her laugh. I do this with one person and it works well.

Sometimes we sense that others complain simply to hear themselves talk, that they don't really want to resolve their difficulties. It appears that they've told the story many times in the past to various people and are stuck in a rut of their own making. In this case, try putting the ball in their court by asking, "What ideas do you have for what can be done?" If they ignore the question and return to complaining, ask again, "What ideas to you have for what could help in this situation?" In other words, refocus them on the question at hand, instead of allowing them to get lost in their tales. Eventually, they will begin to see that they are able to change their view of the situation or their behavior.

2   SPEAKING OF THE FAULTS OF OTHERS: HOW TO MAKE OURSELVES AND OTHERS MISERABLE

Many of us have a well-practiced habit of talking about the faults of others. In fact, sometimes doing this is so habitual that we don't realize we've done it until afterward. Yet, when we examine its effect in our lives, we quickly realize that this habit isn't conducive to either our own or others' happiness.

The Motivation

What lies behind this tendency to criticize others? One of my teachers said, "You get together with a friend and talk about the faults of this person and the misdeeds of that one. Then you go on to discuss others' mistakes and negative qualities. In the end, the two of you feel good because you've agreed you're the two best people in the world."

If we look inside, we may have to acknowledge he's right. Fueled by insecurity, many of us mistakenly think that if others are wrong, bad, or fault-ridden, then in comparison we must be right, good, and capable. Does the strategy of putting others down to build up our own self-esteem work? Not at all.

Another situation in which we speak about others' faults is when we're angry with them. Here we may talk about their faults for a variety of reasons. Sometimes it's to win other people over to our side. "If I tell other people about the argument Bob and I had and convince them that he is wrong and I'm right before Bob can tell them about the argument, then they'll side with me." Underlying that is the thought, "If others think I'm right, then I must be." It's a weak attempt to convince ourselves we're okay when we haven't honestly evaluated our own motivations and actions.

At other times, we may talk about others' faults because we're jealous of them. We want to be respected and appreciated as much as they are. In the back of our minds, there's the thought, "If others see the bad qualities of the people I think are better than me, then instead of honoring and helping them, they'll praise and assist me." Or we may think, "If the boss thinks that person is unqualified, she'll promote me instead." Does this strategy win others' respect and appreciation? Again the answer is no.

Some people "psychoanalyze" others, using their limited knowledge of pop psychology to give someone a derogatory label. Comments such as "He's borderline" or "She's paranoid" make it sound as if we have authoritative insight into someone's internal workings, when in reality we disdain certain traits of theirs because our ego is affronted. Casually psychoanalyzing others can be especially harmful, for it may unfairly cause a third party to be biased or suspicious.

Speaking of others' faults can also be a way to distract ourselves from acknowledging our own painful emotions. For example, if we feel hurt or rejected because a dear one hasn't called us in a long time, rather than feel the suffering nature of our attachment, we criticize our loved one for being unreliable and inconsiderate.

The Results

What are the results of speaking of others' faults? First, we become known as a busybody. Others won't want to confide in us because they will be afraid we'll tell others, adding our own judgments to make them look bad. I am cautious of people who chronically complain about others. I figure that if they speak that way about one person, they will probably speak that way about me too, given the right conditions. In other words, it's hard to trust people who continuously criticize others.

Second, we have to deal with the person whose mistakes we publicized when she finds out what we said, which, by the time she hears it, has been amplified. She may tell others our faults in order to retaliate—not an exceptionally mature action, but one in keeping with our own actions.

Third, some people get stirred up when they hear about others' faults. For example, if one person at an office talks behind the back of another, everyone in the work place may get angry and gang up on the person who has been criticized. This can set off backbiting throughout the workplace and cause factions to form. Is this conducive for a harmonious work environment? Not at all.

Fourth, are we happy when our mind picks faults in others? When we focus on negativities or mistakes, our own mind isn't very happy. Thoughts such as, "Sue has a hot temper. Joe bungled the job. Liz is incompetent. Sam is unreliable," aren't conducive for our own mental happiness.

Finally, by speaking badly of others, we create the cause for others to speak badly about us. This result may occur in this life if the person we have criticized puts us down, or it may happen in future lives when we find ourselves unjustly blamed. When we are the recipients of others' harsh speech, we need to recall that this is a result of our own actions: We created the cause; now the result has come. We put negativity in the universe and in our own mindstream; now it is coming back to us. There's no sense being angry and blaming anyone else if we are the ones who created the principal cause of our problem.

Close Resemblances

There are a few situations in which seemingly speaking of others' faults may be appropriate or necessary. Although these instances closely resemble criticizing others, they are not actually the same. What differentiates them? Our motivation. Speaking of others' faults has an element of maliciousness in it and is motivated by self-concern. Our ego wants to gets something out of this; it wants to look good by making others look bad. On the other hand, appropriate discussion of others' faults is done with concern and/or compassion; we want to clarify a situation, prevent harm, or offer help.

Let's look at a few examples. When we are asked to write a reference for someone who is not qualified, we have to be truthful, speaking of the person's talents as well as his weaknesses so that the prospective employer or landlord can determine if this person is able to do what is expected. Similarly, we may have to warn someone of another's tendencies in order to avert a potential problem. In both these cases, our motivation is not to criticize the other, and we do not embellish his inadequacies. Rather, with a good motivation, we try to give an unbiased description of what we see.

Sometimes we may suspect that our negative view of a person is limited and biased, so we talk to a friend who does not know the person and who can help us see the situation from other angles. This gives us a fresh, more constructive perspective and ideas about how to get along with that person. Our friend might also point out our buttons—our defenses and sensitive areas—that exaggerate the other's defects so that we can work on them.

At other times, we may be confused by someone's actions and consult a mutual friend in order to learn more about that person's background, how she might be looking at the situation, or what we could reasonably expect from her. Or, we may be dealing with a person whom we suspect has some problems, and we consult an expert in the field to learn how to work with such a person. In both these instances, our motivation is to help the other and to resolve the difficulty.

In another case, a friend may unknowingly be involved in a harmful behavior or act in a way that puts others off. In order to protect him from the results of his own mistakes, we may say something to him. Here we do so without a critical tone of voice or a judgmental attitude but with compassion, in order to point out his error so he can remedy it. However, in doing so, we must let go of our own agenda that wants the other person to change. People must often learn from their own experience; we cannot control them. We can only be there for them.

The Underlying Attitude

In order to stop pointing out others' faults, we have to work on our underlying mental habit of judging others. Even if we don't say anything to or about them, as long as we are mentally tearing someone down, it's likely we'll communicate that through giving someone a condescending look, ignoring her in a social situation, or rolling our eyes when her name is brought up in conversation.

The opposite of judging and criticizing others is regarding their good qualities and kindness. This is a matter of training our minds to look at what is positive in others rather than what doesn't meet with our approval. Such training makes the difference between our being happy, open, and loving or depressed, disconnected, and bitter.

Let's try to cultivate the habit of noticing what is beautiful, endearing, vulnerable, brave, struggling, hopeful, kind, and inspiring in others. If we pay attention to that, we won't exaggerate their faults. Our joyful attitude and tolerant speech that result from this will enrich those around us and will nourish our contentment, happiness, and love. The quality of our own lives thus depends on whether we find fault with our experience or see what is beautiful in it.

When we focus on the faults of others, we are missing the opportunity to love them. To reorient ourselves in a positive direction, we need to nourish ourselves with heart-warming interpretations as opposed to feeding ourselves a mental diet of poisonous thoughts.

When we are habituated with mentally picking out the faults of others, we tend to do this with ourselves as well. This can lead to devaluing ourselves. What a tragedy it is to overlook the preciousness and opportunity of our lives and our Buddha-potential.

Thus, we must lighten up, have compassion for ourselves, and accept ourselves as we are in this moment while we simultaneously try to become better human beings in the future. This doesn't mean we ignore our mistakes but that we are not pejorative about them. We appreciate our own humanness and have confidence in our potential and in the heart-warming qualities we have developed so far.

What are these qualities? They are our ability to listen, to smile, to forgive, to help out in small ways. Nowadays, many people have lost sight of what is really valuable on a personal level and instead look to what publicly brings acclaim. We need to come back to appreciating ordinary beauty and stop our infatuation with the high-achieving, the polished, and the famous.

Everyone wants to be loved, to have his or her positive aspects noticed and acknowledged, to be cared for and treated with respect. Everyone dislikes being judged, criticized, and rejected as unworthy. Cultivating the mental habit that sees our own and others' beauty brings happiness to ourselves and others; it enables us to feel affection and to extend love to others. Leaving aside the mental habit that finds faults prevents suffering for ourselves and others. This lies at the heart of spiritual practice, and thus, His Holiness the Dalai Lama says, "My religion is kindness."

We may still see our own and others' imperfections, but our mind is gentler, more accepting, and spacious. People don't care so much if we see their faults when they are confident that we care for them and appreciate what is admirable in them.

Speaking with Understanding and Compassion

The antidote to speaking of the faults of others is speaking with understanding and compassion. For those engaged in spiritual practice and for those who want to live harmoniously with others, this is essential. Pointing out people's good qualities to them and to others makes our own mind joyful; it promotes harmony in the environment, and it gives people useful feedback.

Praising others should be part of our daily life and a component of our Dharma practice. Imagine what our life would be like if we trained our minds to dwell on others' talents and good attributes. We would feel much happier and so would they! We would get along better with others, and our families, work environments, and living situations would be much more harmonious. We plants the seeds from such positive actions on our mindstream, creating the cause for harmonious relationships and success in our spiritual and temporal aims.

An interesting experiment is to try to say something nice to or about someone every day for a month. Try it. It makes us much more aware of what we say and why. It encourages us to change our perspective so that we notice others' good qualities. Doing so also improves our relationships tremendously.

A few years ago, I gave this as a homework assignment at a Dharma class, encouraging people to try to praise even someone they didn't like very much. The next week I asked the students how they did. One man said that the first day he had to make something up in order to speak positively to a fellow colleague. But after that, the man was so much nicer to him that it was easy to see his good qualities and speak about them!

1 RUMINATING:
LIVING IN THE PAST AND FUTURE

We have a precious human life with the potential to develop love, compassion, and wisdom limitlessly. How do we use that potential? What occupies our mind most of the time? When observing our mind, we may notice that much time is spent ruminating about the past and the future. Thoughts and emotions twirl around, seemingly of their own accord, but sometimes we must admit to churning them up or at least not making the effort to counteract them. What do we ruminate about and what effect does it have on our life?

The Past

One big topic of rumination is past hurts. "I was so hurt when my spouse said I was stupid." "I worked so hard for the company, but they didn't appreciate me." "My parents criticized the way I look." We have an excellent memory for all the times others have disturbed or disappointed us and can dwell upon these hurts for hours, reliving painful situations again and again in our minds. What is the result? We get stuck in self-pity and depression.

Another topic is past anger. We repeatedly go over who said what in a quarrel, analyzing its every detail, getting more and more agitated the longer we contemplate it. When we sit to meditate, concentrating on the object of meditation is difficult. But when we reflect on an argument, our concentration is great! In fact, we can sit in perfect meditation posture, looking peaceful externally but burning with anger inside as we single-pointedly remember past situations without getting distracted for even a minute. When the meditation bell rings at the end of the session, we open our eyes and discover that the event we spent the last half hour contemplating is not happening here and now. In fact, we're in a safe place with nice people. What is the effect of ruminating on anger? Clearly, it's more anger and unhappiness.

When we ruminate on feelings of being misunderstood, it is as if we were chanting a mantra, "My friend doesn't understand me. My friend doesn't understand me." We convince ourselves of this; the feeling becomes solid, and the situation looks hopeless. The result is that we feel alienated, and we unnecessarily back away from those we want to be close to because we're convinced they never will understand us. Or, we may spill our neediness all over the other person in an attempt to make him understand us in the way we want to be understood.

All of our ruminations aren't unpleasant, though. We can also spend hours recalling past pleasurable events. "I remember lying on the beach with this wonderful person who adored me," and off we go on a fantastic fantasy. "It was so wonderful when I won that reward and received the promotion I wanted," and the real life situation appears like a movie to our conceptual mind. "I was so athletic and healthy. I could throw a ball like no one else and catch the passes no one else could," and happy memories of past victorious sports events glide through our mind. Consequently, we feel the tinges of nostalgia for a past that is long gone. Or, dissatisfied and anxious, we seek to re-create these events in the future, which leads to frustration because circumstances have changed.

Meditators are no exception to this. We hold on to a wonderful experience in meditation and try to re-create it in future sessions. Meanwhile, it eludes us. We remember a state of profound understanding and feel despair because it hasn't happened since. Accepting an experience without getting attached to it is hard for us. We cling to spiritual experiences in the same way we previously grasped at worldly ones.

The Future

We also spend a lot of time ruminating about the future. We may plan things for hours. "I'll first do this errand, then that, finally the third. Or would it be quicker to do them in the reverse order? Or maybe I should do them on different days?" Back and forth our mind swings trying to decide what to do. "I'll go to this college, do graduate work at that one, and then send out my resume to land the job I've always wanted." Or, for Dharma practitioners, while doing one retreat, we daydream about all the other practice opportunities that lie before us. "This teacher is leading a retreat in the mountains. I can go there and learn this profound practice. Then, I'll go to this other retreat center and do a long retreat. When that is done, I'll be ready for a private hermitage." No practice gets done now because we're too busy planning all the wonderful teachings we're going to receive and retreats we're going to do in the future.

Envisioning the future, we create idealistic dreams. "The Right Man/Woman will appear. He/she will understand me perfectly and then I'll feel whole." "This job will fulfill me completely. I'll quickly succeed and be nationally recognized as excellent in my field." "I'll realize bodhichitta and emptiness and then become a great Dharma teacher with so many disciples who adore me." As a result, our attachment runs wild, and we develop unrealistic expectations that leave us disappointed with what is. In addition, we don't create the causes to do the things we imagine because we're stuck in our head just imagining them.

Our future ruminations may also spin around with worry. "What if my parents get sick?" "What if I lose my job?" "What if my child has problems?" In school, we may not have been very good at creative writing, but in our heads we dream up fantastic dramas and horror stories. This leads to an elevated stress level as we anxiously anticipate tragedies that usually do not occur.

Our worries may zoom around the state of world. "What happens if the economy plummets? If the ozone layer keeps increasing? If we have more anthrax attacks? If terrorists take over the country? If we lose our civil liberties fighting terrorism?" Here, too, our creative writing ability leads to fantastic scenarios that may or may not happen, but regardless, we manage to work ourselves into a state of unprecedented despair. This, in turn, often leads to raging anger at the powers that be or alternatively, to apathy, simply thinking that since everything is rotten, there's no use doing anything. In either case, we're so gloomy that we neglect to act constructively in ways that remedy difficulties and create goodness.

The Present

The only time we ever have to live is now. The only time that spiritual practice is done is now. If we're going to cultivate love and compassion, it has to be in the present moment, because we don't live in any other moment. So, even though the present is constantly changing, it's all we have. Life happens now. Our past glories are simply that. Our past hurts are not happening now. Our future dreams are simply future dreams. The future tragedies we concoct do not exist at this time.

A spiritual practitioner may remember previous illuminating moments and dream of future exotic situations, replete with fully enlightened teachers and blissful insights, but in fact, practice can only occur now. The person in front of us at this moment represents all sentient beings to us. If we're going to work for the benefit of all sentient beings, we have to start with this one, this ordinary person in our everyday life. Opening our hearts to whomever is before us requires discipline and effort. Connecting with the person in front of us necessitates being fully present, not off in the past or in the future.

Dharma practice means dealing with what is happening in our mind at this moment. Instead of dreaming of conquering future attachment, let's deal with the craving we have right now. Rather than drowning in fears of the future, let's be aware of the fear occurring right now and investigate it.

Counteracting Forces

His Holiness the Dalai Lama speaks of counteracting forces for the disturbing emotions. These counteracting forces are specific mental states that we cultivate to oppose the ones that are not realistic or beneficial. Reflection on impermanence and death is an excellent opponent force for worry and for craving. When we reflect on impermanence and our own mortality, our priorities become much clearer. Since we know that death is certain but its time isn't, we realize that having a positive mental state in the present is of utmost importance. Worry can't abide in a mind that is content with what we have, do, and are. Seeing that all things are transient, we stop craving and clinging to them, thus our happy memories and enjoyable daydreams cease to be so compelling.

Recognizing that past turmoil and future rhapsodies are projections of our mind prevents us from getting stuck in them. Just as the face in the mirror is not a real face, the objects of our memories and daydreams are likewise unreal. They are not happening now; they are simply mental images flickering in the mind.

Reflecting on the value of our precious human life also minimizes our habit of ruminating. Our wondrous potential becomes clear, and the rarity and value of the present opportunity shines forth. Who wants to ruminate about the past and future when we can do so much good and progress spiritually in the present?

One counteracting force that works well is realizing that all these ruminations star *Me,* the Center of the Universe. All the stories, tragedies, comedies, and dramas revolve around one person, who is clearly the most important one in all existence, Me. Just acknowledging the power of the mind to condense the universe into Me shows the foolishness of our ruminations. A huge universe exists with countless sentient beings in it, each of them wanting happiness and not wanting suffering just as intensely as we do. Yet, our self-centered mind forgets them and focuses on Me. When we recognize this mechanism, our self-centeredness evaporates because we cannot justify worrying about only ourselves when so many other living beings exist in this universe.

The most powerful counteracting force is the wisdom realizing that there is no concrete Me to start with. It's intriguing to examine: Who is the Me that is the star of all these thoughts? Who is having all these ruminations? When we search, we cannot find a truly existent Me anywhere. Just as there is no concrete Me to be found in this carpet, there is no concrete Me to be found in this body and mind. Both are equally empty of a truly existent person who exists under her own power.

With this understanding, the mind relaxes. The ruminations cease, and with wisdom and compassion, the me that exists by being merely labeled in dependence on the body and mind can spread joy in the world.

4 BEING RESPONSIBLE FOR OUR LIVES: LESSON FROM AN INMATE

Blaming others is one of our favorite activities, especially when we have to account for messy situations or confused emotions in our lives. "I unknowingly got into a bad marriage because my spouse was deceptive." "I have emotional difficulties that lead me to make unwise decisions due to how my family treated me as a child." "I can't find a decent job because of the economy." "I went into that field because others said it would bring sure success, but by the time I graduated, the market was flooded and I couldn't find a job."

Our mind acts is a strange way. When we err, we think it's due to others. When they err, we believe it's because they are bad people. We have lots of sympathy for ourselves and those dear to us and very little for those whom society has declared outcasts—for example, prisoners.

While not negating the force of external circumstances such as prejudice, poverty, and oppression, it would still serve us well to examine the choices we make. What was our role in how our life turned out? Without falling to the extreme of blaming ourselves, we can take responsibility for our lives instead of bemoaning the fact that things never turn out the way we want or expect them to.

Recently, one of the prisoners with whom I correspond told me about his upbringing. As a child, he faced a number of obstacles that many people will not encounter in their lives. Later, he became a drug dealer and at age thirty-two, was arrested and given a twenty-year prison sentence, of which he's in his fourteenth year. He could have blamed his prison sentence and all the ensuing suffering he's experienced in prison on his childhood, but he didn't. When I responded to the letter about his youth with understanding and sympathy but not pity, he replied as follows:

> I've been thinking about personal change. After fourteen years in prison and much soul-searching, I can say with certainty that I have changed for the better. The person that I used to be is gone. If I were to meet him today, I wouldn't like him much.
>
> Prison and the act of having a significant part of your life and your freedom taken from you can be a very sobering experience. It doesn't take a really smart person to figure out that if he did something that cost him fifteen or twenty years of his life, he was doing the wrong thing and needed to change. Some people come to prison with long sentences and drastically change their lives for the better, and some change for the worse. But none leaves prison without changing in some way. I have been fortunate in that I have been able to make some positive and long-term changes in my life.
>
> Although I grew up in less than ideal conditions, I don't hold my parents responsible for the way my life turned out. They did what they did, and right or wrong doesn't matter now. I'm the one responsible for me. Maybe if I had grown up in a different environment, I would have been a different person. But all that doesn't matter; it's all conjecture. It's a waste of time and energy to wonder "what if." My path has been my path. The cumulative total of all previous days of my life and all the people, places, and things that occupied those days has resulted in who and what I am now.
>
> I don't begrudge anyone anything anymore. I used to, until I learned that all that negativity was robbing me of energy and life force. I still sometimes get in moods where I wonder "what if...," but at the heart of my existence, I know that the results of the life that has been me for forty-five years are the results of my learning and different experiences.
>
> The choices I have made since childhood have produced the consequences that have brought me to this point in time. My choices, my consequences, my life, my path. What my parents, grandparents, siblings, cousins, friends, teachers, and all others did in the story of my life is secondary. Ultimately, I am the one re-

sponsible for my life. I blame no one for the direction that my path has gone.

I do think that this path has proven to be a good one despite being at times undesirable and difficult. I have a unique perspective that is an asset and a strength for me. From this perspective and this pool of knowledge that is me, I will live the rest of this life much more positive than I did before. I hope to be an asset to the human race—a part of the solution, not a part of the problem. Now at this stage of life, I can finally think!

What he said touched me deeply. A person who accepts responsibility for his decisions is in a position to effect great change in his life, while someone who continuously attributes his failings and confusion to others digs himself into a hole. If we see ourselves as the victim of conditions others inflicted on us, we are trapped. There is no way to change our situation without changing the other person or undoing the past. How can we think we can control others and make them change when we can't even manage our own mind?

But when we take responsibility for our decisions—even the ones we made when we were young and ignorant, even if those decisions were made in less than optimal circumstances or due to coercion or manipulation by others—then we give ourselves the power to change. We cease getting stuck in the past and instead forgive ourselves and others. We learn from our mistakes and begin to contemplate other alternatives to our present emotional habits or behavioral patterns. We start working with our own mind, bringing forth its wonderful qualities such as love, compassion, and wisdom.

Let's try it!

5 CULTIVATING BENEFICIAL HABITS: PRACTICING DHARMA IN DAILY LIFE

Many people have the misconception that spiritual life or religious life is somewhere up there in the sky—an ethereal or mystical reality—and that our everyday life is too mundane and not so nice. Often people think that to be a spiritual person, we must ignore or neglect our everyday life and go into another, special realm. To me, being a spiritual person means becoming a real human being. Thich Nhat Hanh, a well-known Vietnamese monk, said, "It is not so important whether you walk on water or walk in space. The true miracle is to walk on earth." It's true. In other words, becoming a kind human being is probably the greatest miracle we can perform, and this depends on establishing new mental and emotional habits.

One time I gave a talk in a Hong Kong school to a group of children. One child asked, "Can you bend spoons with your mind?" Another asked, "Has God ever talked to you?" They were very disappointed when I said, "No." I went on to explain that for me a true miracle is becoming a kind human being. If someone has psychic powers but lacks a kind heart, the powers are of no use. In fact, they could even be disadvantageous: People may get very upset if they find all their spoons have been bent!

Setting Our Motivation

How do we cultivate a kind heart? It is not enough to tell ourselves that we should be nice, because telling ourselves what we should or should not be, feel, or do doesn't make us become that way. Filling ourselves with "shoulds" often just makes us feel guilty because we never are what we think we should be. We need to know how to transform our mind. In other words, we must realize the disadvantages of being self-centered. We must truly want to develop a kind heart, not just keep thinking that we *should* develop a kind heart.

In the morning, when we first wake up, before getting out of bed, before thinking about what we will eat for breakfast or which unpleasant person we will see at the office, we can start the day by thinking, "Today, as much as possible I won't harm anybody. Today, as much as possible I will be of service and benefit to others. Today, I will do all actions so that I will become a Buddha for the benefit of all sentient beings."

Setting a positive motivation the first thing in the morning is extremely beneficial. When we wake up, our mind is subtle and delicate. If we set a strong positive motivation at this time, there is a greater chance of it influencing us throughout the day. After generating our positive motivation, we get out of bed, wash, have a cup of tea, and then meditate, recite prayers, or read a Dharma book. By starting the day in this way, we will get in touch with ourselves and become our own friend by treasuring and reinforcing our good qualities.

Sometimes it is difficult to find time to meditate each day. But we always have time to watch TV. We always have time to go shopping. We always have time to get a snack from the refrigerator. Why is it that the twenty-four hours run out when it is time to meditate? When we understand the value and effect of spiritual practice, it will become a high priority in our life, and when something is important, we find time for it. It's good to set up a daily meditation practice of fifteen, thirty, or sixty minutes in the morning. To do that, we may have to sacrifice fifteen or thirty minutes of television the previous evening in order to go to bed a little earlier. But compared to the benefit of practicing the Dharma, missing a little TV is not a big thing. In the same way that we always find time to eat because food nourishes our body, we will find time to meditate and recite prayers because they nourish us spiritually. When we respect ourselves spiritually, we respect ourselves as human beings. Nourishing ourselves spiritually then becomes a very important priority, and having time for it is easy.

In the morning, it is good to begin your meditation session by reciting a few verses and cultivating the altruistic intention to benefit others. Then, do breathing meditation for a while. Sit calmly, experience your breath going in and out, and be aware of the breath nourishing you. Just be in the present moment with the breath, and let all discursive thoughts and worries subside. You may want to chant the mantra of Avalokiteshvara

(Chenresig, Kuan Yin)—OM MANI PADME HUM—or the mantra of the Buddha—OM MUNI MUNI MAHA MUNIYE SOHA. Remember the Buddha's qualities while reciting the mantra because that will inspire you to emulate the Buddha's kindness, wisdom, and skill in your daily activities. Or you may do analytic meditation on the topics described earlier in this book, thinking about the meaning of a particular teaching the Buddha gave and applying it to your own life. This also steers your energy in a positive direction first thing in the morning.

Some people say, "I have children. How can I meditate or say prayers in the morning when they need my attention?" One way is to get up earlier than your children. Another idea is to invite your children to meditate or to chant with you. One time, I was staying with my brother's family and would get up early and meditate. My niece, who was about six at that time, would come into my room. I explained to her that this is a time when I am quiet and do not want to be disturbed, so she would sit near me and draw quietly. Sometimes she would sit in my lap, and when she asked me to sing to her, I would chant prayers and mantras. She really liked this and did not disturb me at all.

It is very good for children to see their parents sit still and be calm. That gives them the idea that they too can do the same. If Mom and Dad are always busy, running around, talking on the phone, stressed out, or collapsed in front of the TV, the kids will also be like this. I don't think this is what parents want for their children. So parents who want their children to learn certain attitudes or behaviors have to cultivate them themselves. Otherwise, how will their children learn? If you care about your children, you have to care about yourselves. You have to be mindful and live a healthy and balanced life for their benefit as well as for your own.

You can also teach your children how to make offerings to the Buddha and how to recite simple prayers and mantras. Once, I visited a friend and her three-year-old daughter. Every morning when we got up, we would bow three times to the Buddha. Then, the little girl would give the Buddha a present—a cookie or some fruit—and the Buddha would give her a present also, a sweet or a cracker. It was very nice for the child, because at age three she was establishing a good relationship with the Buddha and at the same time was learning to be generous and share. When my friend cleaned the house, did chores, or went places with her daughter, they would chant mantras together. The little girl loved the melodies of the mantras. This helped her because whenever she got upset or frightened, she knew she could chant mantras to calm herself down.

Greeting Others

After your morning meditation, have breakfast. Greeting your family in the morning is also part of Dharma practice. Many people are grumpy in the morning. They sit at the breakfast table, poring over the newspaper or reading the back of the cereal box for the umpteenth time. When their bright-eyed children greet them, they grunt and, without looking up, keep reading. When their partner asks them a question, they don't respond, or they glance at them for a moment with a look that says, "Don't bother me." Later, they wonder why they have problems in the family!

Some of us are tired in the morning. But if we generate a motivation of kindness upon awakening, that will help us to overcome the habit of being grumpy and to cultivate a new habit of rejoicing in our fortune. "How fortunate I am to be alive. How wonderful that I am to live with the people I cherish. How fortunate I am to have food to eat today." Reflecting in this manner makes it easier to greet your family with love, to look in their eyes with the genuine affection that's in your heart.

A few minutes chatting warmly with your family in the morning can get both you and them off to a good start for the day. In this way, parents will know their children and won't simply be drill sergeants. It's easy to bark orders at your children, "Get up!" "Brush your teeth!" "Why are you wearing that? It looks terrible! Change clothes!" "Stop playing around and eat breakfast." "Hurry up and get to school. You're late." Many children will react as unruly subordinates when treated in this way. But if you greet your children with love and firmly help them navigate everything in their morning routine, they'll be happier and so will you. Take a few minutes and learn about your children's interests. What do they think about? What are they curious about? Learn about their friends. If you're involved in your children's lives when they're young, you'll be able to instill good values in them. Then, when they're older you'll be more confident that they'll be able to deal with situations, and you won't worry so much.

Going to Work

Before you go out the door to work or school, pause for a moment to set your motivation. Think, "I'm going to work not simply to earn a living but to benefit others. May everyone who receives the product or service my company produces be well and happy." Put your kind heart into the goods or services so that you feel a connection with the people who will receive the results of your labors.

Generate a kind heart toward your colleagues. "Today, I will try to be friendly and cooperative with the people I work with. I want to benefit them by creating a pleasant working environment." Then go into your work place and say "Good morning" to everyone and greet them with a smile. This will make a big difference in your working relationships. In addition, others will meet a happy person first thing in the morning instead of a grumpy, unpleasant person who may become more demanding as the day goes on.

Furthermore, think, "I will use whatever happens at work today as part of my Dharma practice." Generate the motivation to be open and receptive to whatever you experience that day. If someone praises you, remember that your qualities came due to the kindness of your teachers and others and in that way avoid becoming arrogant. If someone criticizes you unfairly, realize that he is miserable, and instead of taking the comment personally, care about the suffering of the other person. On the other hand, if someone criticizes you for a mistake you made, acknowledge it, apologize, and learn from the error. There's no need to become defensive or angry.

Throughout the day, remember that you don't want to harm anybody, that you want to be of service to them, and that you seek to do all actions for the ultimate enlightenment of yourself and others. To remind yourself of this, you may want to use a frequent event as a trigger to call you back to your motivation. For example, every time you stop at a red light, instead of being irritated and thinking, "Why is this red light so long? I'm late for work!" think, "Today, I want to have a kind heart toward others." In this way, the red light becomes an opportunity to remember the kind heart. When the telephone rings, instead of rushing to pick it up, first think, "May I be of service to whomever is on the line." Then answer the phone. Every time your pager goes off, calmly come back to the kind heart, and then respond to the call. A friend told me that her trigger to remember the kind heart was her children calling, "Mommy! Mommy!" Since her children frequently called her throughout the day, she became familiar with the kind heart and was much more patient with her children.

Cultivating Mindfulness

As you go about your life, instead of living on "automatic," try to be aware of what you are thinking, feeling, and saying. When we live on automatic, we go through life reacting to things but never really experiencing life. This is why so many people feel out of touch with themselves. For example, most people travel to work every day. When they arrive at their workplace, if somebody asked them, "What did you think about during the half hour you were driving?" they probably couldn't answer. Most of us are unaware of what is going on inside us. Yet a lot is going on, and this influences how we feel about ourselves and how we relate to other people.

The antidote to living on automatic is to cultivate mindfulness. Mindfulness means being aware of what we are thinking, feeling, saying, and doing each moment. It also means being mindful of our ethical values and of the kind heart, so that we can live according to them in our daily lives. By cultivating this awareness, we will no longer simply react to things and then wonder why we are so confused and exhausted at the end of the day. If we are mindful, we will notice that we have a kind heart and will enrich it and let our actions flow from it. Or, we may become aware that we are upset, irritated, angry, or are on the verge of scolding somebody. If we realize that, we can come back to our breath and come back to our kind heart, instead of putting negative energy into the world.

Mindfulness also entails becoming more aware of how we interact with our environment. We realize that we live in an interdependent world and that if we pollute our environment, we affect ourselves, our children, and other living beings. Because we are mindful of being kind, we will curtail the ways in which we pollute the environment. We will take public transport or carpool when going to work or school instead of using up gasoline in a car by ourselves. We will recycle the things we use: paper, cans, plastic containers, bottles, glass jars, newspaper, and cardboard. We know that if we throw these in the garbage, we are destroying our planet and are affecting other beings in a negative way. Thus, we will re-use plastic bags and paper bags when we go to the supermarket. In addition, we will not leave our air conditioners or heaters on when we are not home and will not use products such as styrofoam, whose production releases many pollutants into the air.

If the Buddha were alive today, I think he would establish vows that we have to recycle and avoid wasting resources. Many monastic vows arose because lay people complained to the Buddha about what monks or nuns did. Each time this happened, the Buddha would establish a precept in order to curb the detrimental behavior. If the Buddha were alive today, people would complain to him, "So many Buddhists throw out their tin cans, glass jars, and newspaper! They use disposable cups and plates, plastic forks and spoons. These not only make more garbage but also cause the destruction of many trees. They do not seem to care about the environment and the living beings in it!" The Buddha would see the truth in what they said and would establish a vow saying that we have to recycle and curtail consumption.

Mindfulness also enables us to be aware if we are about to act destructively in our daily life. Mindfulness realizes, "I'm getting angry," or "I'm being greedy," or "I'm feeling jealous." Then we can apply the various antidotes the Buddha taught to help us calm our minds. For example, if we discover we are annoyed and anger is arising, we can stop and look at the situation from the other person's point of view. When we do this, we recognize they want to be happy, and because they aren't happy, they are doing that action we find objectionable. Then instead of harming them out of anger, we will be more compassionate and understanding and will work with them to negotiate a mutually beneficial agreement.

How do we do this when a quarrel is just about to start or we're already in the middle of one? We have to practice beforehand, in our meditation practice. In the heat of the situation, it is difficult to remember what the Buddha taught if we haven't practiced it previously when we were calm and peaceful. In the same way that a football team practices on a regular basis, we need to meditate on patience and to recite inspiring verses daily to get well trained. Then, when we encounter a situation in daily life, we will be able to use the teachings.

Another practice to increase mindfulness and help you remember your motivation is to offer your food before eating. This practice was described in Part I, Chapter 4. If you are in a restaurant, while your companions or business associates continue to chat, you can mentally offer the food to the Buddha without anyone knowing. When you're with your family, if everyone is agreeable, it's nice to recite the food offering verses before eating. Once when I stayed with one family, their six-year-old son led us in reciting the prayer while everyone held hands. It was very touching.

When you eat, eat mindfully. Be aware of the effort other people put into growing, transporting, and preparing the food. Realize your interdependence with other living beings and how much benefit you have received from them, such as the food we eat. If you reflect in this way before eating, you will feel happy and grateful and will eat more mindfully, too.

It is important to eat in a dignified manner. Sometimes we see people in a cafeteria line who haven't paid for the food yet and are already shoveling it in. This is eating on automatic; it resembles a dog that runs to the bowl and slurps up the food. When we reflect before eating and offer our food to the Buddha at our heart, we eat more slowly and are more relaxed.

Coming Home

Before you walk into the door of your home, pause and come back to your motivation, "I'm going to see the people I care about now. I will be mindful and cultivate good relationships with them because I cherish them." Then open the door and step into your home. If you have a spouse and children, greet them lovingly. Look into their eyes so they know you care about them. So often we take those with whom we live for granted, thinking that because we are so close, they just have to put up with the way we are. This way of thinking is detrimental. Instead, by interacting with your family with a kind heart, everyone will be happier. You will be better able to share and support each other.

In the evening, instead of becoming mesmerized in front of the computer or dropping onto the bed and falling asleep, take a few minutes to sit quietly. Reflect on what happened during the day. Looking back over your day, ask yourself, "What went well today? Did I act with a kind heart?" Notice the instances when you acted kindly and rejoice. Dedicate that positive potential for the enlightenment of yourself and others.

In reviewing the day, you may discover that you were angry, jealous, or greedy. You may not have realized it at the time, but later you don't feel so good about what you felt, thought, said, or did. To purify this, develop regret and do some purification practice so you can forgive yourself and let that negative energy go. In this way, resolve any uncomfortable feelings or misdirected actions that may have arisen during the day.

Having done this, you will sleep more peacefully. When you lie down, rejoice that you were able to live one more day with the Dharma. Pray that others may be free from suffering and have this fortune as well. Make kindness part of your motivation for sleeping, "I will sleep now to rest my body so that tomorrow I can continue progressing on the path to enlightenment and continue to benefit sentient beings in whatever way, big or small, that I can." Imagine the Buddha on your pillow and put your head in the Buddha's lap when you go to sleep. You may want to imagine gentle light flowing from the Buddha into you. This is very comforting and helps you to remember the Buddha's good qualities and to have better dreams.

Practicing Dharma is not difficult or time consuming. We always have time; there are always twenty-four hours in a day. If we direct our mind positively, we can transform whatever action we do into the path to enlightenment. In this way, the Dharma becomes part of our life in an integrated way. Getting up in the morning is Dharma, eating and going to work are Dharma, sleeping is Dharma. By transforming our attitude in the midst of daily activities, our life becomes greatly meaningful.

IV THE SPREAD OF THE
BUDDHA'S TEACHINGS

In the preceding sections, we looked at the essence of the Buddha's teachings and how they apply to our lives in the twenty-first century. But we may wonder what the origins of the teachings were, and how they were passed down in a pure form to our day. Why are there many Buddhist traditions, and what are they? How is Buddhism practiced in various countries? These will be discussed next.

1 THE LIFE OF THE BUDDHA:
AN INSPIRATION FOR US ALL

He gave expression to truths of everlasting value and advanced the ethics not of India alone but of humanity. Buddha was one of the greatest ethical men of genius ever bestowed upon the world.

> —Albert Schweitzer, French scholar, theologian,
> philosopher, and winner of the Nobel Prize

The lives of truly remarkable people improve society so greatly that we're grateful that they lived. In addition, their biographies inspire us and show us how we too can traverse hardships and benefit others. In the Buddha's life story, we find circumstances with which we can identify. We can then relate these to our lives and our efforts to become better people.

The Buddha was born as Prince Siddhartha in the Shakya royal family of Kapilavastu, now located in modern-day Nepal, around 560 B.C.E. His mother had several auspicious dreams before his birth, and as a newborn, he is said to have taken seven steps and declared, "This shall be my last rebirth."

Some people find great joy in hearing about the many miraculous occurrences that surround the Buddha's birth and life and that demonstrate his spiritual achievements. Other people are skeptical about these accounts for such things haven't been scientifically explained yet.

We could debate endlessly about this, but to do so is to miss the point. What's important is that we improve the quality of our lives by following a correct path. Hearing the life story of another person can be an inspiration and example for our own spiritual growth. Thus, if you find the stories of miraculous events inspirational and helpful in your life, that's good. If you don't, that's fine, too. Concentrate on the parts of the life story that have meaning for you.

The Buddha's mother died a week after his birth, and he was raised by his stepmother, Prajapati. A wise man told the Buddha's father, the king of Kapilavastu, that this child would be an exceptional personage—either a great king with political, economic, and social power or a great sage with the wisdom and compassion to lead others on the spiritual path.

The king wanted the best for his child, and in his eyes, that meant having power over people and wealth. He didn't see the value of his child being religious. Thus, the king created what he considered the best possible environment for his child's growth—one in which the child, Siddhartha, had everything that money could buy. Anything disagreeable was excluded from the child's environs, nor was he allowed beyond the palace walls, for there he might contact something unpleasant.

As a child, Siddhartha was very compassionate and successful in both intellectual pursuits and athletics. He married well and had a child. In all ways he fulfilled the expectations of his family and society and was what they would call "a success."

One day, Siddhartha ventured beyond the protected environment of the palace with his charioteer. There he saw an old person—wrinkled, frail, bent over, and in pain. This was a new sight for the sheltered prince, since elderly people had been banned from the palace. When he questioned the charioteer about this person, he learned that the aging process happens to all of us, without choice. Returning to the palace, he was melancholy, his dream bubble of perfect worldly happiness shattered by the first pinprick.

Another day he ventured out with his charioteer, this time seeing a sick person on the street. Again, upon asking, he learned that all of us are subject to illness, although we don't desire it.

The third time he went out, he saw a corpse. When the charioteer explained that death is inevitable and all of us must leave our bodies, enjoyments, and loved ones, the prince was horrified. He was beginning to wonder what life was all about, considering that without choice, we experience aging, sickness, and death. What use were all his beautiful possessions, his power and prestige, if they couldn't prevent these? He realized that even his family and friends, though they loved him immensely, could prevent neither his sickness, aging, and death nor their own.

On the fourth excursion outside the palace walls, Siddhartha saw a mendicant dressed in simple clothes, with few possessions. The charioteer explained that this was someone who had left behind the distractions of family life and was seeking the meaning of life and the solution to its problems.

One evening after a gala affair, when the dancing girls were asleep, snoring, with their hair disheveled, Siddhartha decided he had to seek a solution to the dissatisfactory nature of life. He saw no sense in devoting his life to pleasures of the senses if one day he must die and leave them all, never having actualized his full potential as a human being.

He kissed his sleeping wife and child good-bye and, with his charioteer, left the palace. Discarding his exquisite royal clothes and jewelry, he donned simple garb and cut his hair. Seeking to learn the answer to life's mysteries, he went in search of a teacher.

For some years he studied with the most renowned meditation masters of his time and achieved perfection in all they taught. Still, his mind wasn't free from attachment, anger, and ignorance. To change this, he decided to follow a path of extreme ascetic practices. With five companions, he meditated for six years, eating only one grain of rice each day. Although he attained high states of samadhi, his mind still wasn't completely free. He learned through his own experience that torturing the body isn't the source of spiritual realizations.

Enlightenment

Giving up extreme asceticism, he regained his physical strength and went to Bodhgaya, in northeastern India. There, he sat beneath a bodhi tree and vowed not to rise until perfect enlightenment had been attained.

Then, tradition says that Mara, the chief of the demons, sent his forces to disrupt Siddhartha's meditation. We may regard Mara as an external being who creates hindrances or as that part of our own minds that is still confused, clinging, and unclear. The story of the ensuing battle has many messages for us.

Mara first sent aggressive warriors to disrupt Siddhartha, but the meditator transformed their weapons into a rain of flowers. The fear and anger in our minds can be conquered by love.

Mara next sent his daughters, voluptuous and enchanting, to lure the bodhisattva from his resolve and disturb his concentration. However,

Siddhartha transformed them into hideous hags who fled in humiliation. Our desires have no strength when we look beyond the superficial appearance of what we're attached to.

Lastly, Mara challenged the bodhisattva's right to be there, questioning if he had enough positive potential. Siddhartha touched the ground, and the goddess of the earth appeared, testifying to his great accumulation of positive potential. Our doubt is dispelled when we're firmly grounded in reality. Defeated, Mara departed.

During the night, the bodhisattva continued to meditate, gradually removing the last vestiges of the stains of ignorance and selfishness, and at dawn, he became a fully enlightened Buddha, one who has cleansed all defilements from his mind and who has developed all good qualities to their fullest.

Teaching the Dharma

At first the Buddha appeared hesitant to teach, for would anyone understand the extraordinary experience he had had? Then the great celestial beings, headed by Brahma, came to request him to teach, saying surely there were people with little dust on their wisdom-eyes who could benefit.

The Buddha journeyed to Sarnath, where he knew his five companions, the ascetics, were staying. Seeing him, they were disgusted that he had relinquished his asceticism, and they vowed to ignore him. However, as the Buddha drew nearer, their preconceptions and anger dissolved in the face of his radiant compassion and wisdom. They welcomed him, and he gave his first teaching.

This first discourse was on the four noble truths. The ascetics gained understanding of them, requested ordination, and eventually became arhats. In this way, the Sangha community was formed.

For forty-five years, the Buddha traveled throughout northern India, teaching and giving counsel. People from all walks of life became his disciples and benefited immensely from practicing what he taught. At one point he returned to Kapilavastu and taught the Dharma to his family. His father, now understanding the benefit of his son's spiritual practice, was pleased with him and learned from him. The Buddha's own son became a monk.

After the demise of his father, the Buddha's stepmother, together with five hundred Shakya women, requested ordination. At first the Buddha refused, probably because he didn't want his stepmother to make such a decision due to her grief at the loss of her husband.

Prajapati was determined, however. She and the five hundred other women followed the Buddha the many long miles to Vaishali, shaved their heads, and donned the saffron robes to show their sincerity. Ananda, the Buddha's attendant, questioned the Buddha whether women were able to become arhats, and the Buddha responded that they were. The Buddha decided to grant them ordination, and the order of nuns was formed. The Buddha's wife also later became a nun.

In many ways the Buddha was a social revolutionary of his time. He spoke strongly against ritual for ritual's sake, thus forcing people to reconsider the purpose of the mass of Brahmanical rituals they performed. He also spoke out against the discrimination and prejudice of the caste system and didn't allow it within the Sangha community. He insisted that all people be treated equally. Respect was to be given to those who had been ordained longer and to those with realizations, not to people because they had been born into a certain social class.

Considering the inferior position of women in ancient Indian society, the Buddha shocked many people by acknowledging women's spiritual capacity. He allowed women to leave the home, where, according to societal custom, they were always under the care and custody of men: first their fathers, then their husbands, and in old age their sons.

There were many eminent nuns who attained arhatship, and their teachings are in the scripture entitled the *Therigatha*. Some people say that the Buddha initially declined to ordain women and then reluctantly changed his mind, implying that maybe he was making a mistake. However, the Buddha also declined to teach the Dharma at first and later changed his mind. No one says that he made a mistake by doing that!

Also, contrary to the authoritarian governments that existed in India at that time, the Buddha favored a more republican and democratic system, which he instituted in the Sangha community. After monastics were ordained for ten years, they were considered stable in their practices and were designated "elders." The elders met together to discuss, form, and enforce policies in the Sangha communities.

The "law" of the Sangha community was the monks' and nuns' vows set down by the Buddha. When the first disciples took ordination, there were no specific vows. The precepts came into being as some monks and nuns acted in ways that either harmed themselves or others or were offensive to others. When such a situation was brought to the Buddha's attention, he would then say that in the future, his ordained disciples should refrain from such an action.

The principal vows are not to kill a human being, not to steal, not to lie about one's spiritual attainments, and not to have sexual relations. Other vows regulate monastics' physical appearance and dress, behavior with other monastics, and etiquette. The Sangha are also not to take intoxicants of any kind.

The Buddha had many lay disciples from all classes, in addition to the communities of monastics. The relationship between the ordained and the lay was one of mutual benefit and appreciation. The "job" of the Sangha— the monastics—was to practice the teachings as well as they could, to be an inspirational example to others, and to teach and guide others. To do this, they were to live a simple life. They were not to engage in agriculture or business for their livelihood, because these occupations require a lot of time that could be used for study and meditation, and they could also arouse attachment.

Therefore, each morning the monastics went on alms rounds to collect their daily food at the homes of the laity. Although this has sometimes been translated as "begging," it isn't. The Sangha would not ask for food, nor was anyone obliged to give food to them. They would silently pass the homes, and those people who saw value in the Sangha's spiritual pursuits and wanted to help them happily gave to them.

The ordained ones were not parasites on society. In fact, they had a crucial role to play in it for they practiced the teachings, and by integrating the Dharma in their mindstreams, they improved their conduct and wisdom. They could then teach these methods to the laity, as well as demonstrate that it's possible to become more peaceful, compassionate, and open people.

Nevertheless, that doesn't mean that because people are ordained, their behavior is automatically impeccable. They are training. Most Buddhists— whether they are ordained or lay—are not yet Buddhas! They are trying to become enlightened. Although the path that the Buddha described is perfect, the humans who practice it aren't always that way.

When the Buddha was eighty, after forty-five years of teaching and guiding others, he passed away at Kushinagar. This is also called the Buddha's *parinirvana*. Rather than appoint a successor and establish a hierarchy, the Buddha encouraged his followers to let the Dharma—the teachings he gave—be their guide. In doing this, he emphasized the importance of each individual's sincere practice and expressed his wish that the Sangha live together democratically.

2 BUDDHIST TRADITIONS: FINDING WHAT SUITS US

In the first rainy season after the parinirvana, the First Council was held at Rajagriha. The five hundred arhats who attended recited and compiled the sutras—the teachings given by the Buddha. For several centuries after that, the sutras were memorized and passed down orally to each succeeding generation.

The Buddha spoke to a wide range of people from every social, educational, and economic background. His followers varied in disposition, interest, and inclination. Thus, the Buddha taught according to the specific group present at each discourse, using words and concepts suitable for them.

The various teachings he gave later developed into two principal traditions: the Theravada and the Mahayana. The Theravada contains the teachings spoken by the Buddha to people who were interested in being free from cyclic existence and attaining liberation. These sutras were passed down orally until the first century B.C.E., when they were written down in Ceylon and became what is known as the Pali Canon.

The Mahayana teachings were given by the Buddha to an audience with strong interest in the bodhisattva's path to Buddhahood. After the Buddha's passing away, the Mahayana teachings weren't practiced publicly but were passed down privately from teacher to disciple. Tradition has it that some Mahayana sutras were taken to another land to be cared for until conditions were right for their widespread propagation in our world. From the first century B.C.E. onward, the Mahayana sutras began to appear publicly, and this way of practice became more widely known.

Buddhism is remarkably flexible in the external forms it takes. Thus, it has adapted to the culture of each country where it has taken root. While the Buddhist traditions vary in terms of on which texts they chiefly rely, which practice they emphasize, and the outward manifestations of the practice, they are all united in that they are the teachings of a very skillful and wise teacher, the Buddha.

The various traditions maintain the purity of the Buddha's doctrine. This is important, because to progress along the path we must follow it correctly. It would be very harmful to change the teachings, for that would amount to making up our own path to enlightenment rather than following the guidance of someone who has already achieved it.

When first coming to Buddhism, many people are bewildered by the variety of Buddhist traditions. In the next few chapters, we'll look at the major traditions existing today, and how they developed historically. As this is a vast subject, only the most prominent traditions are discussed: Theravada, Pure Land, Ch'an (Zen), and Tibetan Buddhism.

We may personally be more attracted to one tradition and focus upon it. However, we can't say this tradition is better than the others or that it's the most suitable for everyone else. Such sectarianism is extremely harmful. Instead, we can appreciate Buddhism even more because it acknowledges and accepts everyone's different dispositions, interests, and cultures.

3 THERAVADA, THE TRADITION OF THE ELDERS: BUDDHISM IN SRI LANKA AND SOUTHEAST ASIA

Saffron-robed monks, fragrant flower offerings in temples, melodious chanting in Pali, and the deep peace of silent meditation—these are images evoked by the Theravadin tradition.

The Theravadin tradition was widely practiced in India after the Buddha's passing away. By the third century B.C.E., it was established in current-day Pakistan and Afghanistan. It took root in Central Asia in the early centuries C.E. However, Muslim invasions in the eleventh and twelfth centuries virtually extinguished Buddhism in the Indian subcontinent and in Central Asia.

In the third century B.C.E., King Ashoka of India sent missionaries to Ceylon (now called Sri Lanka), where Buddhism became firmly established. The Theravadin tradition still flourishes there. From India and from Ceylon, the Theravada spread to Southeast Asia and is presently strong in Thailand, Cambodia, Laos, and Burma, even though the Communist governments of several countries in that region have suppressed Buddhism. In recent years the Theravadin tradition has become more widely practiced in Malaysia and Singapore.

In the nineteenth century, Western intellectuals became interested in the Theravadin tradition. Nowadays, it attracts people from all walks of life, and Theravadin monasteries, Dharma centers, and retreat sites have been established throughout the West.

Based on the Pali Canon, the Theravadin tradition presents Buddha's teachings by first explaining the four noble truths, the three higher trainings, and the noble eightfold path. These have been discussed in previous chapters. The Theravadin tradition states that while all beings—male and fe-

male—may become arhats, only a comparatively small number will become Buddhas who turn the Dharma wheel—that is, who give teachings in
a world where Buddhism is not yet present. In our eon, there will be one
thousand Buddhas who turn the Dharma wheel, of which Shakyamuni
Buddha is the fourth. The 996 Buddhas-to-be are now bodhisattvas. Thus,
because the rest of us won't become Buddhas, we should aim to become
arhats, those who are free from cyclic existence and have attained nirvana. (The difference between Buddhas and arhats was explained in Part I,
Chapter 2, "The Four Noble Truths.")

People wishing to attain nirvana can take refuge and the five lay precepts. They can also take monastic vows. In the Theravadin tradition full
monastic ordination is considered an important condition for the attainment of nirvana.

There is a considerable difference between Sangha and lay people in
their way of practicing the Dharma in Asian Theravadin countries. The
monks keep their precepts purely, study, meditate, and dedicate the positive potential they create for everyone's welfare. Because the Sangha's practice benefits society as a whole, the laity happily supply daily
requisites—food, clothing, shelter, and medicine—to the monks.

This view of the roles of Sangha and laity is changing as the Theravadin
tradition takes root in the West. Most Western lay Buddhists are interested
in meditation, and many meditate daily before and after going to work.
They go to Dharma centers for their annual vacation. Some even take several months leave from their jobs to participate in lengthy retreats. In the
West, Dharma teachers are both ordained and lay, men and women.

The Theravadin Method of Practice

The more I studied *satipatthana* (mindfulness meditation), the more
impressed I became with it as a system of mind training. It is in
line with our Western scientific attitude of mind in that it is un-
prejudiced, objective, and analytical. It relies on personal, direct
experience and not on anyone else's ideas or opinions...it gets you
out of the rut and bondage of yourself, your prejudices, your clichés,
your blindness, and your self-opinionatedness, to set you free to
see and prove a real world.

Dr. E. Graham Howe, MB. BS. DPM.
Eminent British physician

In all Buddhist traditions, two principal qualities are developed in meditation: meditative quiescence and special insight. Generally, meditative quiescence is practiced first to free the mind from its internal chatter and to develop concentration. In the Theravadin tradition, the breath is taken as the object of meditation, and one trains the mind to be alert and focused on the sensation of the breath in each moment.

When initially trying to concentrate, the mind is cluttered with mental noise, like being trapped in a room with fifteen radios, all blaring on different stations. Several techniques are applied to help solve this problem. One may relax each part of the body and, while doing so, let go of a distracting thought. With another technique, one simply acknowledges the presence of the thoughts and emotions that arise but doesn't give them attention and energy. In this way, they settle of their own accord. Another technique instructs one to recite the syllables "Bud dha" on the in and out breaths to help focus one's concentration.

Apart from formal sitting meditation, one does walking meditation. Walking slowly, one concentrates on each movement and sensation involved in lifting, moving, and placing the feet. In fact, in all daily actions—sitting, standing, lying down, talking, or whatever—one tries to be aware of each minute action and event.

By focusing the mind on the sensation of the breath in sitting meditation and on each movement in walking meditation, one becomes more aware of the richness of the present moment. In addition, one's concentration is removed from the daydreams and barrage of thoughts that feed the afflictions. The mind remains tranquil, and one fully experiences every event in life.

The practice of special insight, or vipassana, develops an acutely perceptive and discerning state of mind that can directly perceive the ultimate reality, selflessness, or lack of a solid self-identity. In the Theravadin practice, this is done by means of the four foundations of mindfulness: mindfulness of the body, feelings, mind, and phenomena.

Closely examining these four, one becomes aware of three characteristics: their transience, their problematic or suffering nature, and their lack of a solid self-identity. By observing and examining the breath, the physical and mental feelings, the various consciousnesses, and the mental factors in each moment, one realizes there is no little person somewhere inside one's head running the show. We are selfless, without a solid self-identity that needs to be pleased and protected.

Special insight is also developed outside of formal sitting meditation. By being acutely aware of each action, feeling, and thought, one examines who is doing and experiencing these things. Finding only a continuous stream of mental and physical events, without a concrete personality or self who is the boss, one understands selflessness.

Combining special insight with the concentration of meditative quiescence, one is able to cleanse the mindstream of all afflictions and the karma that cause suffering. Attaining liberation, one becomes an arhat.

The meditation on loving-kindness, or *metta*, is also popular in the Theravadin tradition. One begins by thinking, "May I be well and happy," and gradually spreads this good feeling to friends, strangers, and enemies. Considering each in turn, one thinks, "May they be well and happy." One must let these words resonate inside oneself so they become one's own attitude. Meditative quiescence can also be developed through meditation on loving-kindness.

In the West, Theravadin practice is popular with people who wish to calm their uncontrolled thoughts and emotions and to focus on positive attitudes. Many people in the business world have found breathing meditation extremely helpful in this respect. Meditation on loving-kindness has helped them improve relationships with their families and colleagues. This 2,500-year-old tradition is certainly applicable and beneficial today!

4 MAHAYANA, PURE LAND, AND ZEN: BUDDHISM IN THE FAR EAST

Buddhism first came to China from Central Asia in the first century C.E. Later, it was brought from India by both sea and land routes. By the fourth century, bhikshu and bhikshuni ordination lineages were established in China. In following centuries, Chinese pilgrims continued to bring a wealth of Buddhist texts from India to China.

Pre-Buddhist China was influenced by the indigenous philosophies of Confucianism and Taoism. When it entered China, Buddhism was flexible and adapted its external forms to the existing culture. For example, Confucianism emphasized etiquette, respect for elders and teachers, filial piety, and proper behavior. When Buddhism came to China, the monks emphasized the sutra on the kindness of the parents, as this complemented values important in Chinese culture. Similarly, etiquette and formal ceremonial procedures were stressed in Buddhist monasteries.

Taoist practice contained breathing exercises and techniques to develop the subtle energies of the body. Chigong, a system of exercises working with energies in the body, had also existed in China for many centuries. The Buddha had taught breathing exercises and meditation to control the body's subtle energies as well.

Thus, when the Indian meditation master Bodhidharma went to China, he improved upon the already existing practices there and developed a set of exercises to improve the monks' health. In this way, the exercises of the martial arts came to be practiced in Buddhist monasteries. However, contrary to popular films, Buddhist monks didn't spend their days flipping opponents over their shoulders! They engaged principally in the study and practice of Buddha's teachings.

The Buddhist texts brought to China by Indian missionaries and Chinese pilgrims weren't initially systematized. Over time, people became unsure how to resolve seeming discrepancies between sutras and how to practice the teachings in this vast treasure of literature.

Thus, in the seventh century there were spontaneous attempts in China to organize the Buddhist teachings. Groups grew up around various monks, each of whom chose a particular sutra or group of sutras as the central point of their study and practice. These groups later evolved and became Buddhist traditions, each one passed down by its own lineage of masters. Eight major traditions developed in China, as well as some minor ones. The eight principal traditions were:

1. San-lun, which followed the Madhyamaka (Middle Way) philosophical school of Indian Buddhism.
2. Fa-hsiang, which followed the Yogachara (Chittamatrin, Mind Only) philosophical school of Indian Buddhism.
3. Satyasiddhi (Ch'eng-shih), a Theravadin tradition.
4. Hua-yen, which was based on the *Avatamsaka Sutra* and dealt with an array of metaphysical concepts for contemplation.
5. T'ien-t'ai, which took the *Lotus Sutra* as foremost and presented a balance between meditation, philosophical study, and good deeds.
6. Third Period (San-chieh-chiao), a method for purification based on strict observance of monastic vows and charitable actions.
7. Ch'an (Jap. Zen), which emphasized meditation and the *Lankavatara Sutra*.
8. Pure Land, in which practitioners strove to be reborn in the pure lands of Amitabha Buddha or Maitreya Buddha.

Aside from these eight major traditions, Chen-yen (True Word), a tantric tradition, existed in China in the eighth and ninth centuries.

In the Great T'ang Persecution of 842–5 C.E., Buddhism was severely repressed in China. All of the traditions except for Ch'an and Pure Land were essentially destroyed, although their influence remains and there is interest in them today. After 845, Ch'an and Pure Land became the principal Chinese Buddhist traditions, both of them studying the Middle Way and Mind Only philosophies. Since the sixteenth century, Ch'an and Pure Land practices have been blended together in many Chinese monasteries.

From China, Mahayana Buddhism spread to Vietnam beginning in the second century C.E. and to Korea in the fourth century. Ch'an became prevalent in both places, although in Vietnam Pure Land and Theravadin traditions became popular as well.

In the sixth century, most Chinese Buddhist traditions reached Japan via Korea. In the twelfth and thirteenth centuries, many new traditions proliferated in Japan. This occurred because people were bewildered by the vastness of the Buddha's teachings and sought a single effective practice in which to engage.

During this time, two Pure Land traditions separated from T'ien-t'ai. Of these, the Jodo-shin-shu, the True Pure Land Sect, emphasized the family as the center of religious life. It began the custom of married priests, who take vows and lead religious practices in temples. The temples are passed down from father to eldest son.

Although Ch'an (Zen) came to Japan as early as the seventh century, it became popular in the twelfth. Many Zen traditions exist, but Rinzai and Soto became the most well known.

In the thirteenth century, the Nichiren tradition, based on the *Lotus Sutra,* appeared. Shingon, the Japanese tantric tradition, was also revitalized around this time.

In the Meiji Restoration of 1868, the Japanese government decreed that all Buddhist clergy be allowed to marry. During the Japanese occupation of Korea in the early twentieth century, non-celibate priesthood was introduced. But now most Korean Sangha follow the ordination vows of monks and nuns, which necessarily include celibacy.

Post-war Japan has seen the rise of many small groups, each with its own way of practice. Some have integrated the pre-Buddhist Shinto beliefs into their system; others have adopted a Christian bent. If we're interested in Buddhist practice, we should examine well the teachings of these groups to determine if their interpretation is faithful to the Buddha's teachings.

From Japan in particular, Zen and Nichiren-sho-shu have spread to Western countries. Zen has become very popular in the West, where people attend meditation sessions and retreats. Some Zen centers have begun social welfare programs as well: hospices to help the terminally ill or people with AIDS.

Having seen the historical development of Buddhism in East Asia, let's look at the two most prominent traditions there: Ch'an (Zen) and Pure Land.

Pure Land

The melodious and soothing chant of "Namo Amito Fo" (Homage to Amitabha Buddha) resonates in many Chinese temples and homes. The figures of Amitabha, flanked by his two chief attendants, the bodhisattvas Avalokiteshvara and Mahasthamaprapta, inspire many. For centuries, the simplicity of the Pure Land practice, which centers upon the recitation of Amitabha's name, has attracted devotees from all classes of society.

The Pure Land tradition is rooted in the *Sukhavati-vyuha Sutra,* as well as several other sutras describing how to be reborn in Amitabha's pure land, Sukhavati (Blissful Pure Land or Western Paradise). The Amitabha practice existed in India, although it wasn't as prominent there as in East Asia. In the second century C.E. the *Sukhavati-vyuha Sutra* was translated into Chinese, and in the early sixth century it became very popular.

This practice fit in very well with Chinese culture. Taoist practice revolved around attaining longevity, and since Amitabha Buddha is the same as Amitayus, Buddha of Infinite Life, people became interested in the Pure Land practice. Similarly, the Taoist concern with longevity was transferred to seeking rebirth in Amitabha's pure land. The practice of reciting *dharani* (efficacious syllables) was already popular in northern China, making it easy for people to switch to chanting Amitabha's name.

These conditions enabled people to easily adopt the Pure Land practice. In addition, times were hard in China, and people welcomed a technique that was simple and direct. Pure Land wasn't presented as an elitist practice, but one in which everyone, the illiterate as well as the scholarly, could participate.

The long-term goal of this practice is to attain enlightenment for the benefit of all beings. The immediate goal is to be reborn in Sukhavati, the Blissful Pure Land, in the next life. This pure land is not included in the six realms of cyclic existence because once beings are born there, they'll definitely attain enlightenment and will never be reborn in cyclic existence again. Of course, once people become Buddhas in Sukhavati, they'll manifest in our world to lead others to enlightenment.

Why is rebirth in a pure land desirable? In the human world, sincere practitioners often face many obstacles: They have to work long hours and thus have less time for concentrated practice; there is crime and anger in society; people have to worry about money to support their families; distractions from the media lure their attention away from practice.

In the pure lands such as Sukhavati, these hindrances don't exist. Everyone practices Dharma, and all the conditions—physical, social, economic, and so on—are conducive to realizing the path. Because attaining enlightenment is easy there, rebirth in Sukhavati is desirable. In addition, Sukhavati is unusual among the many pure lands because it's easier to go there: ordinary beings who have neither direct perception of emptiness nor the full-fledged altruistic intention (bodhichitta) can be reborn there.

Sukhavati Pure Land came into existence as a result of the practice of a bodhisattva monk, Dharmakara, who many eons ago had the wish to create a place where other beings could easily practice Dharma. He made a series of vows in which he promised to establish this pure land when he became a Buddha and described the means by which others could be reborn there. Dharmakara then learned the Dharma from a previous Buddha, generated the altruistic intention, and completed the practices of meditative quiescence and special insight. In this way, he became the Buddha Amitabha, and by the power of his positive potential and wisdom, Sukhavati came into being.

How can people be reborn in Sukhavati? Some people believe that having strong faith in Amitabha and reciting his name are sufficient. Then, by Amitabha's power, they'll be led to the pure land when they die.

This is a rather simplistic view and raises the question, "Buddha said no one can save us but ourselves. We must practice Dharma and transform our own minds. Isn't it contradictory to say one needs to have only faith and Amitabha will do the rest?"

Yes, this is contradictory. While Amitabha can inspire and guide people, they must practice. The Sukhavati sutras set out this practice: ethical conduct, purification of destructive actions, generation of the altruistic intention (bodhichitta), concentration, and meditation on the qualities of the Buddha and the pure land. Then, with a heartfelt aspiration, one dedicates the positive potential from one's practice to be reborn in Sukhavati in order to attain enlightenment for the benefit of all others.

Faith is an adjunct to meditation. It arises not through blind belief or desperation but through knowing the qualities of the Buddha, Dharma, and Sangha.

The practice of reciting Amitabha's name can be used to develop the above qualities. For example, by reciting "Namo Amito Fo" while thinking of Amitabha's altruistic intention, one admires bodhichitta and will develop it in one's life. By focusing on the sound of Amitabha's name, one eliminates distractions and develops concentration. One can gain meditative quiescence by using a visualized image of Amitabha and the pure land as one's meditation object. Special insight on selflessness is developed by meditating on the emptiness of inherent existence of Amitabha and oneself. Thus, we see that the Pure Land practice is very rich and goes beyond merely reciting Amitabha's name.

During daily life activities one continues the recitation to remind oneself of the qualities of the Three Jewels. While walking or driving, one can develop mindfulness on the sound of Amitabha's name. Remembering that ethical conduct is a principal cause for rebirth in a pure land, one becomes mindful of what one thinks, says, and does.

Some of the confusion about whether recitation of Amitabha's name is sufficient practice arose because the Chinese term *nien-fo* has several meanings. *Nien* can mean: (1) concentration or meditation, (2) a moment of time, or (3) vocal recitation. In India, Amitabha practice centered upon meditation. In China, it emphasized recitation of his name. The same Chinese term can be applied to both.

Also, when masters stress the importance of relying on Amitabha, one shouldn't think Amitabha is an all-powerful god who can do everything. According to Buddhism, a Buddha is omniscient but not omnipotent. It's impossible for anyone to be omnipotent. The power of a Buddha and the power of sentient beings' karma are equal. If one hasn't created the cause to be reborn in Sukhavati by doing positive actions, Amitabha can't magically make one go there.

There are various ways to regard Amitabha, according to the level of one's understanding and practice. The external Buddha Amitabha resides in the pure land. However, the internal Buddha Amitabha is an enlightened mind that our present mind can become by practicing the Dharma. Neither the external nor the internal Amitabha is a concrete, inherently existent personality. In fact, the more one understands selflessness, the more one has a proper understanding of who Amitabha is.

As with all Buddhist practices, this one can be done on several levels, depending upon the understanding of the practitioner. Recitation and generating devotion to Amitabha is beneficial for people who lack education or who don't have the time or interest to learn Buddhist philosophy. For them, it provides direction in their lives and refuge during stressful times. By reciting Amitabha's name and thinking of him, they create positive potential. People with a more comprehensive understanding of the Buddhist path to enlightenment apply this to the Pure Land practice and thus attain profound realizations.

The Pure Land tradition is well suited for people who find that devotion inspires them to abandon afflictions and develop their good qualities. Invigorated by their confidence in Amitabha, they'll practice the Dharma and gain the realizations of Amitabha in their own mindstreams.

Ch'an (Zen)

Zen is traced to a teaching the Buddha gave by silently holding up a golden lotus. The general audience was perplexed, but the disciple Mahakashyapa understood the significance and smiled subtly. The implication of this is that the essence of the Dharma is beyond words. In Zen, that essence is transmitted from teacher to disciple in sudden moments, breakthroughs of understanding.

The meaning that Mahakashyapa understood was passed down in a lineage of twenty-eight Indian patriarchs to Bodhidharma. Bodhidharma, an Indian meditation master, strongly adhered to the *Lankavatara Sutra*, a Yogachara text. He went to China around 470 C.E. and began the Ch'an tradition there. It spread to Korea and Vietnam, and in the twelfth century became popular in Japan.

Ch'an in Sanskrit is *dhyana*, which means "meditative concentration." All the early Indian missionaries and Chinese monks were meditation masters. Meditation was one of many practices the Buddha gave instruction in—ethical discipline, generosity, patience, and wisdom were others—and the Ch'an tradition arose from the wish of some practitioners to make meditation their focal point.

An underlying principle in Zen is that all beings have Buddha-nature, the seed of intrinsic Buddhahood. Some Zen masters express this by saying that all beings are already Buddhas but that their minds are clouded over by afflictions and obscurations. Their job, then, is to perceive this Buddha-nature and let it shine forth without hindrance.

Because the fundamental requirement for Buddhahood—Buddha-nature—is already within everyone, Zen stresses attaining enlightenment in this lifetime. Zen masters generally don't teach in depth about rebirth and karma, although they accept these.

According to Zen, there is no need to avoid the world by seeking nirvana elsewhere. This is because, first, all beings already have Buddha-nature, and second, when they realize emptiness, they'll see that cyclic existence and nirvana are not different.

Zen is acutely aware of the limitations of language, and Zen practice is geared to transcend these limitations. Experience is stressed, not mere intellectual learning. Thus, associating with an experienced teacher is important. The Zen teacher's duty is to bring the students back to the reality existing in the present moment whenever their fanciful minds get involved in conceptual wanderings. This is illustrated by lively anecdotes of Zen masters catching their students off guard and thus breaking through the confusion of their unrealistic views.

Sanzen, daily consultation with the teacher, is conducted during periods of intense meditation. Brief but to-the-point discussion with the spiritual master can not only trigger insight in the student but also gives the teacher the opportunity to access and validate the student's experiences in meditation. Having a profound personal relationship also provides for the mind-to-mind transmission of Dharma experience from teacher to student.

Zazen, sitting meditation, is a key practice. The two major Zen traditions, Soto and Rinzai, have a slightly different approach to this. Soto Zen teaches "just sitting" in which one focuses on the nature of the mind. Soto emphasizes "original enlightenment" and doesn't distinguish between the means and the end. Instead of constantly trying to achieve something, one is encouraged to just be and to be aware of that.

Meditative quiescence is developed in Soto Zen by just sitting, thus concentrating the mind single-pointedly. Based on confidence that sitting is the perfect expression of inherent perfection, or enlightenment, the practice of special insight involves total awareness of the body sitting in each moment.

Rinzai Zen employs the *koan* (Chinese: *kung-an*) to develop special insight. Different koans are used by each teacher, and each koan serves a different purpose. But basically, these short puzzles, such as, "What was the appearance of your face before your ancestors were born?" or "What is the sound of one hand clapping?" challenge one's usual way of relating to one-self and to the world. One may use logic to approach the koans, but real understanding transcends verbal explanations and depends on insight into one's ultimate nature.

The point of contemplating a koan isn't to get the right answer. Rather, it's to confront people with their preconceptions. Becoming frustrated be-cause the usual intellect and emotions can't make sense of the koan, the sleeping mind will wake up. A koan can't be answered by the discursive superficial mind but only by deep insight. Practitioners of the Rinzai tradi-tion gain meditative quiescence by focusing the mind on the koan. They gain special insight by answering it.

When one finally breaks down a mental barrier and suddenly penetrates into the meaning of reality, the resulting experience is called *satori*. A deep intuitive experience such as satori is not a goal in itself but is rather a call to further practice. After a satori, one still needs to reveal one's Buddha-nature even more. Although Zen talks about "sudden enlightenment," it seems like realizations are gained in a gradual manner. What is sudden is the collapsing of the last barrier in a series and the experience of new insight.

In daily life, Zen practitioners develop mindfulness in all actions, espe-cially while working. Reflecting this, Ch'an monasteries in China altered one aspect of the vows of individual liberation and assigned Sangha mem-bers to do manual labor such as agriculture. This originated from the needs of the monasteries to support themselves in ninth-century China. Never-theless, working can also be a tool for developing mindfulness and being attentive to all one does, says, and thinks. While working mindfully, Zen practitioners cultivate the same inner silence experienced during sitting meditation. Work also reminds one that nirvana isn't to be sought else-where but is actualized in the here and now.

Although Zen is a Mahayana tradition, many of its spiritual masters don't give extensive and explicit teachings on how to generate the altruistic intention. Instead, they stress meditation and the arising of wisdom. The idea behind this is that once the ego's preconceptions are cut and emptiness realized, the underlying unity of all people and things will become readily apparent. Then, compassion and love for others will naturally arise.

As the Zen tradition spread in East Asia, it included various cultural elements in its practice. For example, in Japan, flower arrangement, the tea ceremony, and gardening became ways to practice Zen in daily life. These activities also integrate into Buddhism the appreciation of nature and beauty found in Shinto, a pre-Buddhist religion in Japan.

The Japanese esteem the strict discipline of the warrior, so Zen practice emphasizes sitting in perfect meditative position and "conquering" the pain of an aching back and sore knees. Accordingly, in some monasteries, the meditation supervisor hits slouching or sleeping meditators with a stick to awaken them.

Zen emphasizes simplicity in external appearances as well as in meditation practice. This was initially a reaction against the over-intellectualization of Chinese and Japanese scholars. In addition, many people were overwhelmed by the variety of Buddhist practices and sought an explicit and direct approach.

Nowadays, many peoples' homes and lives are often cluttered with the physical and mental paraphernalia of life in a technological society. The seeming simplicity of Zen appeals strongly to them. They enjoy entering an uncluttered meditation hall and appreciate the discipline of meditation. This is part of Zen's appeal in modern society.

5   INTEGRATION OF SUTRA AND TANTRA: TIBETAN BUDDHISM

Buddhism was first brought to Tibet in the seventh century by two Buddhist princesses—one from Nepal, the other from China—who married the Tibetan King Songtsen Gampo. However, Buddhism wasn't widely established in Tibet until the eighth century, when the monk Shantarakshita and the tantric yogi Padmasambhava came from India, bringing with them the Mahayana and tantric teachings. In the eighth century, Ch'an Buddhism also came to Tibet from China.

Controversy soon arose among the Buddhist groups. Ch'an practitioners taught a kind of blank-minded meditation in which all conceptual thoughts, be they virtuous or not, were to be extinguished. Masters trained in the Indian tradition stressed first having a correct conceptual understanding and then going beyond that to direct experience in meditation. Ch'an asserted that realizations could come suddenly and spontaneously. Indian Buddhism stated that a gradual process, including good works as well as meditation, was necessary to become enlightened.

In India, debates were held to refute misconceptions of non-Buddhists and to enhance Buddhists' understanding of the teachings. To settle the controversy, the Tibetan king proposed a debate, during which the Indian debater Kamalashila defeated the Chinese proponent of Ch'an. Since that time, Tibet has followed Indian Buddhism.

In the eleventh century, several more lineages of teachings came to Tibet from India. These were called the New Translation schools, in contrast to the Nyingma or Old Translation school of Padmasambhava. Among the New Translation schools were the Kadam, begun by the Indian monk and scholar Atisha who taught widely in Tibet; the Sakya, founded by Drokmi, a Tibetan who went to Vikramashila University in India; and the Kagyu, traced to Marpa, a Tibetan who studied at Nalanda University in India and practiced under the guidance of the great yogi Tilopa. The fourteenth-century scholar and monk Tsongkhapa drew from all the above lineages, but principally from the Kadam, and his followers became the Gelug tradition.

These four Tibetan traditions are essentially the same, the principal difference being one of lineage. The basic meditations on the determination to be free, the altruistic intention, and the wisdom realizing emptiness are similar in all four traditions.

Similarly, they all do certain preliminary practices. Nyingma, Kagyu, and Sakya students often do the preliminaries during a three-year retreat, while Gelug students spread them out over a longer period of time. In Gelug, a three-year retreat is for more advanced practitioners who meditate continuously on a particular manifestation of the Buddha.

The four Tibetan Buddhist traditions vary somewhat in their approach to the practice in the final stages of the tantric path and have different vocabulary to describe the meditation. But, as His Holiness the Dalai Lama, the religious and political leader of Tibet, repeatedly stresses, all of the traditions come to the same point, and enlightenment can be attained through any of them.

The lineage of monks' and nuns' vows is the same in all four Tibetan traditions. However, spiritual masters may be either ordained or lay. When they teach, some lay masters dress in maroon robes, similar to but not exactly the same as monks' and nuns' robes. Lay teachers often marry and have a family, but all monastics in the Tibetan tradition take a vow of celibacy.

Lama, Geshe, and Rinpoche

People are often confused by Tibetan titles, which can be employed in a variety of ways. In the Gelug tradition, the title *lama*, which may be translated as "teacher," is generally given to respected masters. However, anyone who has disciples is technically a lama. In the other three traditions, "lama" is designated to any one who has completed a three-year meditation retreat. Thus, lamas may have very diverse abilities and training.

The title *geshe* is conferred on one who has undergone extensive philosophical training and is like a Tibetan Ph.D. in Buddhist studies.

Rinpoche is a title meaning "precious" and is given in two circumstances. The predominant one is for the recognized reincarnation of a previous spiritual master. In addition, disciples may respectfully refer to their personal teacher and to the abbot or retired abbot of a monastery as "Rinpoche."

His Holiness the Dalai Lama often advises spiritual seekers to select teachers not by their titles but by their spiritual qualities. Many good practitioners shun titles while some unqualified people parade about with many titles. We should not be influenced by superficial appearances but examine to see if prospective teachers have genuine spiritual qualities.

Bringing Buddhism to Tibet

The pre-Buddhist Bon religion in Tibet influenced some of the external forms that Buddhism took there, and it was, in turn, influenced greatly by Buddhism. The tradition of offering incense on mountain peaks came from Bon and was given a Buddhist meaning. So were prayer flags, brightly colored pieces of cloth strung on a line. Buddhist prayers and mantras are printed on them now, and the wind carries these good wishes throughout the world.

The colorful and elaborate dancing expressing religious themes was also adapted from pre-Buddhist culture. The large drums, cymbals, and horns are indigenous to Tibet, although the *vajra (dorje),* bell, and small hand drum are tantric implements from India.

When importing Buddhism from India, Tibetans emphasized producing accurate translations and standardizing technical terms. Teams of Indians and Tibetans translated as much of the Sanskrit Canon from India as possible. As a result the Tibetan Canon is larger than the Chinese, although it doesn't contain all the Indian texts. The Chinese Canon has some texts not translated into Tibetan.

Many Indian commentaries on the sutras were translated into Tibetan, and the Tibetans soon added commentaries of their own. They imported the Indian system of debate and their love for clear and concise explanation of the teachings, and this is apparent in Tibetan Buddhism today.

Tibetan Buddhism is found in the northern areas of modern India and in some areas in Nepal. In addition, it spread to Mongolia and Manchuria beginning in the thirteenth century. Since the Chinese Communist takeover of Tibet, which forced thousands of Tibetans to flee into exile in India and Nepal, Tibetan Buddhism is more accessible to others. Although Buddhism has been severely suppressed under the Chinese Communist government, Tibetan refugees have re-established monasteries in India. In addition, lamas and geshes have gone to many Western and Asian countries where Dharma centers have sprung up.

Vajrayana

Tibetan Buddhism is a combination of both sutra—the Theravadin and general Mahayana teachings—and tantra (Vajrayana or Mantrayana), which is a unique branch of the Mahayana. The Buddha taught the tantras to an audience of high bodhisattvas. These teachings weren't for public practice because they were suitable for the dispositions of only some people.

Thus, the tantric lineages were passed down privately from master to a few disciples in India. Vajrayana practice became known more publicly starting in the sixth century. Although it spread throughout the Buddhist world, Vajrayana survived principally in Tibet and in the Japanese Shingon tradition.

Buddhist tantra and Hindu tantra should not be confused. Although the two have similar terminology and breathing exercises, they differ vastly in their philosophy, practice, and results.

Tibetan masters stress that their students follow the teachings of all three—Theravada, Mahayana, and Vajrayana—all of which are found in Tibetan Buddhism. In the practice common with the Theravada, a practitioner takes refuge in the Triple Gem, observes ethical conduct, and develops the determination to be free. On this basis, one develops the altruistic intention to attain enlightenment for the benefit of all beings, which is the special emphasis of the Mahayana. One trains in the view of selflessness through the philosophical tenets of both the Theravada and Mahayana. Having developed to this extent, one then may take a tantric empowerment.

Taking an Empowerment

An empowerment or initiation is conferred by a qualified spiritual master. In a specific ceremony, the teacher describes how to meditate and the disciple does the meditation at that time. Merely being present in the room or drinking consecrated water isn't sufficient to receive the empowerment. One must follow the instructions of the master and meditate. Some empowerments involve taking only the bodhisattva vows, while others require the tantric vows as well.

Some people believe that empowerments are given as blessings and that teachings on the determination to be free, the altruistic intention and the wisdom realizing emptiness (the three principles of the path) are advanced teachings. They think empowerment is some sort of magical blessing and crave to drink blessed water or be tapped on the head by sacred objects. This is not the correct understanding of Vajrayana.

The three principles of the path are basic teachings that all Buddhists can listen to and practice. They form the foundation and give people the motivation and understanding of the Dharma necessary to take empowerments.

Sometimes a master will give an empowerment in the form of a blessing so that people can form a karmic connection with the Vajrayana. Nevertheless, people must still concentrate at the time of the ceremony.

The purpose of an empowerment is to plant the seeds for future enlightenment and to introduce one to the meditation practice of a specific manifestation of the Buddha. Therefore, empowerments should be taken with a serious, respectful attitude. Afterward, students must ask the master for instructions on the vows and commitments and then keep these as purely as possible.

In addition, students can request teachings on the actual practice—or sadhana—of that Buddha figure. The spiritual master will explain the philosophy of the Vajrayana and how to do the meditation of that Buddha figure or deity. By practicing according to instruction, one receives benefit.

Some people collect empowerments as if they were medals to pin on their coats. They boast to their friends how many holy masters have blessed them and how many empowerments they've received. But they don't do the daily meditation of these Buddha figures, nor are they mindful of what they do, say, or think while they're at work and at home.

Such people won't advance in their practice for several reasons. First, their motivation is a worldly one—for prestige. Good motivations for practicing Dharma are to prepare for future rebirth, to attain liberation from cyclic existence, or to become enlightened to be able to benefit others. True practitioners don't brag about their practice. As long as one isn't enlightened, there's nothing to boast about, and when one is enlightened, one is humble and doesn't brag.

Second, such people don't observe cause and effect in their daily lives and thus continually create causes for unfortunate rebirths. To advance on the path, it's essential to live ethically and to be kind to others.

Third, they don't engage in the practice of the deities whose empowerments they received. Without putting effort into practice, there's no way to advance. Serious practitioners humbly follow the instructions given by their spiritual masters and, in this way, attain realizations.

Meditating on Buddhist Deities

We may wonder why Vajrayana deals with so many Buddha figures, or deities. All Buddhas have the same realizations. However, for our benefit, they appear in a variety of physical forms in order to emphasize certain aspects of their realizations to us.

For example, Avalokiteshvara (Chenresig, Kuan Yin, Kannon) specifically shows compassion. One form of this Buddha figure has one thousand arms, symbolizing continuously reaching out in a diversity of ways to help others. Another deity, Manjushri, is deep yellow in color, representing the brilliance of wisdom. He is shown holding the sword of wisdom to illustrate the necessity of cutting through all obscurations to enlightenment. A female Buddha, Tara, is green, which reminds us of the green of spring and summer and thus represents prosperity, growth, and success in spiritual practice.

Tantric meditation involves working with the imagination. The mind has a tremendous capacity for visualization and imagination. In fact, it is involved when we become angry, attached, or proud, for we visualize telling someone off or imagine being with the person to whom we are attached. In Vajrayana, this imaginative capacity of the mind is transformed and used in a positive way to approach enlightenment.

At the beginning of a tantric practice, one meditates on the emptiness or absence of any solid personal identity. From the spaciousness of emptiness, one imagines that the wisdom realizing emptiness manifests in the physical form of a Buddha figure, e.g., Avalokiteshvara. By simultaneously meditating on the appearance of oneself as Avalokiteshvara and the emptiness of inherent existence, a practitioner creates the causes to attain both the body and the mind of a Buddha.

Identification with Avalokiteshvara rouses the practitioner from feelings of inadequacy. By identifying with an ideal, the future Buddha one can become, a person adopts those characteristics and relates to others in a more loving and compassionate way now.

Recitation of mantras is done while imagining oneself in the pure form of a Buddha figure. A mantra is a prescribed set of syllables consecrated by a Buddha. It contains the essence of an enlightened being's realizations. Recitation of mantras can settle and concentrate the mind. In daily life, people chatter, worry, or hum melodies in distraction. Reciting mantras transforms this already existing tendency into a beneficial practice leading to a focused and purified mental state.

In the Vajrayana, meditative quiescence is developed on the image of oneself as a deity, or on certain syllables or implements imagined at various points in the deity's body. Special insight into emptiness is gained by focusing not only on the emptiness of oneself and the deity at the beginning of the meditation, but also on the emptiness of oneself as a Buddha during the meditation.

Tibetan Buddhism emphasizes the importance of finding a qualified spiritual master and then following his or her Dharma instructions properly. This is especially true for those doing the technical meditations of Vajrayana practice.

Tibetan Buddhism is spreading to Western countries. People are attracted by its step-by-step teachings to develop love, compassion, and altruism, as well as its extensive and precise teachings to realize emptiness. Others are attracted by Vajrayana's use of imagination and transformation. But whatever tradition toward which a person is inclined, it's important to be sincere, honest, and humble in one's practice.

6   BUDDHIST TEMPLES AND DHARMA CENTERS: WHAT HAPPENS THERE?

The figure of the Buddha serenely sitting in meditation—this is the first thing we see upon entering a Buddhist temple. Our minds relax as we look at the peaceful figure, for we are finding that quiet and caring place inside ourselves. When we bow before a statue of the Buddha or place offerings on the shrine, we aren't propitiating an idol made of bronze; we're getting in touch with and respecting those parts in ourselves that resemble the Buddha.

A Buddhist temple is a place to remember the heights that human potential can attain. It's a place to recall that in spite of whatever disturbing emotions or problems we have in our lives, it's possible to transcend them. In the temple, we also remember that all beings—our friends, enemies, and strangers—have the intrinsically pure Buddha-nature. Our mood changes as we tap into these understandings.

Depending upon whether we have grown up in a Buddhist culture or not, many of the things in the temple may seem familiar or foreign to us. Also, each temple is slightly different according to which Buddhist tradition it follows.

In Theravadin temples the figures of the Buddha are usually sitting in meditation, or reclining as when he passed away (parinirvana). Often there is a bodhi tree in the courtyard, reminiscent of the bodhi tree under which Siddhartha attained enlightenment in Bodhgaya. Outside the main temple, a four-faced statue is sometimes seen. Some people mistakenly call this the "four-faced Buddha," but actually it's a statue of four-faced Brahma, a Hindu deity who was part of Sri Lankan and Thai culture from pre-Buddhist times.

In Chinese temples, especially those of the Pure Land tradition, there are several Buddha figures. Included among these may be: the Medicine Buddha, showing the healing capacity of the Buddhas; Amitabha, reminding us of Sukhavati Pure Land, where he presides; Avalokiteshvara (Kuan Yin), the manifestation of the compassion of all Buddhas; Manjushri on a lion, who embodies the wisdom of the Buddhas; or Samantabhadra on an elephant, signifying the bodhisattva's practice and strong determination.

Although externally these Buddhas and bodhisattvas appear in different forms, as represented by the statues or paintings, they all have the same realizations of compassion, wisdom, and so on. Because the realizations of Buddhas exist in their minds, which we can't see with our senses, they appear in forms that express their realizations and the special way in which they help others. Just as art expresses the thoughts and feelings of the artist in a physical form, the forms of the Buddhas symbolically express their realizations and ways of helping.

Chinese temples also may have images of fierce-looking, bearded figures called Dharma protectors. Dharma protectors are either bodhisattvas or mundane deities who have pledged to protect the Dharma and its practitioners. The figures of the Dharma protectors remind us to protect the Dharma inside of us by practicing it purely and not for worldly gain.

There is often a shrine in Chinese temples where the ancestral tablets of deceased relatives are placed. The names are written on red paper, as red is an auspicious color in Chinese culture. Relatives and friends place incense or fruit before the tablets, indicating their good wishes for the departed ones. The ancestral shrine isn't of Buddhist origin. It comes from Chinese culture.

Japanese temples, particularly those of the Zen tradition, have simple shrines, while Tibetan temples are generally elaborate. This reflects the cultures of the countries. Tibet, for instance, is a vast and sparsely-populated country of mountains and plateaus where one can see nothing for miles. It seems natural, then, that the Tibetans would build colorful temples full of Buddha figures.

Some people erroneously say the forceful-looking figures in Tibetan temples are demons. This is not the case at all. In line with the Vajrayana emphasis on transformation of ordinary emotions into divine wisdom, these figures represent wisdom and compassion demolishing self-grasping, ignorance, and selfishness, the roots of all our sufferings.

Buddhist devotees often bow or prostrate before the figures of the Buddhas and bodhisattvas in a temple. This is a sign of respect, not only to the beings who have become Buddhas and who thus have done what we want to do but also to the future Buddhas that we'll become.

The candles, fruit, incense, water, and so forth offered on the shrine also show our respect and admiration for Buddhahood. The Buddhas don't seek our prostrations or offerings: A fully enlightened one doesn't need an apple to be happy. Rather, making offerings is a way for us to train our minds to be joyful when giving. We offer because *we* need to: To develop spiritually, we must diminish our attachment and miserliness.

Almost anything can be offered on the shrine, as long as it was procured in ways that didn't harm others. Thus, we avoid offering meat or things obtained by overcharging customers. Flowers, lights, incense, and water are the most common offerings. People can arrange them in any way they consider beautiful and offer as much or as little as they wish.

Our motivation for offering is important. We shouldn't think we are "getting in good" with the Buddha so the Buddha will make us rich and powerful. First, holy beings can't be bribed. Second, we must create the cause to have happiness, and this comes through acting ethically and cultivating a kind heart.

Therefore, before offering, it's advisable to cultivate the motivation to benefit others and to attain liberation or enlightenment. By offering, we'll create positive potential, which will bring not only temporary benefits but spiritual realizations as well.

Activities at the Temples

Temples are centers of religious and cultural activities. People may come at any time to meditate or pray, and there are daily services that are chanted. The purpose of chanting is to guide our minds in a positive direction. By reflecting upon the meaning of what is being said, we can understand it better and integrate it in our hearts. Because we should contemplate while we chant, it's more appropriate to call this practice "chanted meditation."

The style of the services and chanting varies from one tradition to the next, depending on the culture of the country. Theravadin services are chanted in Pali, while the Chinese, Vietnamese, and Tibetans chant in their own languages. Now that Buddhism is coming to the West, a variety of languages are used at Dharma centers. Some recitations are now chanted in

English, Spanish, and so on, and this will surely continue because people prefer to understand the meaning of the verses they are chanting. Buddhists will certainly adapt Buddhism's external forms and services to the cultures of Western countries.

Chanting is often done to the accompaniment of bells, gongs, and drums. These are used to help the participants keep the melody of the chants and are also an offering of music to the enlightened ones.

Buddhist teachings and meditation classes are held at the temples. The importance of receiving Dharma teachings can't be stressed enough, for without learning we don't know how to practice properly.

In Asian cultures, some lay people take the Dharma for granted and are content simply to go to the temple, make offerings, and participate in a chanting service, without doing any other practices. They feel that teachings are for monastics, who have dedicated their lives to practicing the Dharma.

Fortunately, this is beginning to change, and more Asian lay people are interested in receiving the vast and extensive teachings. Teenagers and young adults are especially interested in learning the Dharma and practicing it during meditation sessions and in their daily lives. Asian Buddhists are now establishing Sunday schools for their children, rather than teaching them about Buddhism at home.

Western practitioners—be they monks, nuns, or lay people—appreciate Dharma teachings very much and will even travel great distances to obtain them. They go to the Dharma centers (Buddhist temples) especially to receive teachings and meditate, for they want to learn as well as practice.

Some temples organize social welfare projects, such as setting up schools, youth groups, orphanages, clinics, and old people's homes. His Holiness the Dalai Lama has encouraged more of these kinds of activities, for then we not only meditate on altruism, but we also practice it.

It would be wonderful if lay followers took the initiative in establishing more social welfare projects. Traditionally, monastics haven't been very active in this area, as the Buddha emphasized that they practice deeply, without getting distracted by too many external activities. If the Sangha doesn't study and practice well, they won't be able to pass on the teachings or gain realizations.

To learn the Buddha's teachings thoroughly and to practice them correctly takes time. Although lay people are dedicated to this, because of their families and jobs, their time is limited. Therefore, the specialty of the Sangha is learning, practicing, and teaching others. However, these activities aren't limited to the Sangha for there are many lay followers who are excellent practitioners and teachers. If Sangha members regard social and educational projects as part of their practice of compassion, they should definitely engage in them.

7 BUDDHIST FESTIVALS AND RITES:
HOLIDAYS, BIRTH, MARRIAGE, AND DEATH

Buddhism follows the lunar calendar, so full and new moon days are times of special activities. Many lay followers go to the temples to participate in chanting services, pray, and create positive potential by making offerings. Some take the eight precepts for the day. Many Chinese temples offer a vegetarian lunch to the public on those days.

The full and new moon days also mark the purification and confession days of monastics. They recite and review their vows and renew their determination to keep them purely in the future.

The most important Buddhist holiday is Vesak, the day the Buddha became enlightened. This is celebrated on the fifteenth day of the fourth month in the lunar calendar, which usually falls in May or June. People often take the eight precepts on this day and flock to the temples to participate in services.

Some traditions say Vesak is also the day of the Buddha's birth and passing away, while others celebrate the Buddha's birthday on the eighth day of the fourth lunar month. On this day, Buddhists of some traditions will symbolically wash a statue of the Buddha with scented water to recall when the gods bathed the Buddha after he was born.

Seven weeks after Vesak is the anniversary of the Buddha's first teaching—also called the "turning of the Dharma wheel." This marks the time when the Buddha taught the four noble truths in Sarnath.

Tibetan Buddhists distinguish four special days in the Buddha's life, of which the first two are Vesak and Turning the Dharma Wheel. On the fifteenth day of the first lunar month, they celebrate the day that the Buddha demonstrated miraculous powers to non-believers, resulting in their following the Buddhist path. The fourth holiday is celebrated a week after the end of the rainy season retreat. This marks the Buddha's return to our world after having gone to a god realm for three months to teach the Dharma to his mother.

The yearly rainy season retreat, lasting for three months during the summer, has been observed by monastics since the time of the Buddha. In India, many insects and animals multiply during the summer monsoon rains. To prevent their accidental deaths, the Buddha had his followers stay in a specific area during this time, instead of moving from one locality to another.

This is a time of retreat for the Sangha, during which they aren't allowed to accept robes, bedding, and so forth. A special ceremony marks the end of the rainy season retreat. This is followed by the *kathina* ceremony, in which the laity offers new robes to the Sangha, for at the end of the monsoons their possessions are worn out by the dampness.

In Chinese Buddhism, the anniversaries of various bodhisattvas are also celebrated. These days mark occasions referred to in the scriptures when bodhisattvas were born, first generated the altruistic intention, or made special vows to help others.

As Buddhism spread to many countries, it conformed to the cultural activities of those places. As a result, some cultural activities continued as before, only they were given a Buddhist flavor. One example is Lunar New Year, a holiday observed by many pre-Buddhist cultures. In Tibet, Buddhist prayer services were added to the general new year's celebration, and people were encouraged to make elaborate offerings to the Buddhas, bodhisattvas, and Dharma protectors as an auspicious way to begin the new year.

In addition, the Great Prayer Festival (*Monlam*) was begun in Lhasa in the early fourteenth century, attracting Sangha and lay people from all over Tibet. His Holiness the Dalai Lama or other great practitioners would teach during this time, and candidates for the geshe degree would debate. Unfortunately, the Communists occupying Tibet have virtually stifled the Great Prayer Festival, but the Tibetans in exile continue to celebrate it.

Marriage, Birth, and Death

There is no formal "baptism" ceremony for children born in Buddhist families. However, parents may make offerings and prayers and request chanted meditations for the benefit of their newborn child. When children are old enough to understand the Dharma, they may take refuge and "officially" become Buddhists.

In Buddhism, marriage is considered a secular matter. In fact, the Buddha prohibited monastics from matchmaking or performing marriage ceremonies. This was to help them to preserve their celibacy vow and to avoid taking time from study and meditation.

Sometimes lay Buddhists perform marriages, including a discussion of Buddhist beliefs in the ceremony. Or, after a secular ceremony Buddhist couples go to the temple to make offerings or sponsor a prayer session to create positive potential for a happy marriage. At this time, monastics perform chanted meditations and pray for the couple's lives to be happy and beneficial for themselves and others.

During times of difficulty, people often request the Sangha to recite the sutras, do chanted meditations (*puja*), and pray for them. However, Buddhists don't pray to the Buddha as an all-powerful god and ask him to solve their problems. Buddhists believe that no one, even the Buddha, is omnipotent. If someone were all-powerful, he or she surely would have eliminated the world's problems by now.

Nor must we ask the Buddha to have mercy on us and cease punishing us for our harmful deeds. Buddhas have infinite compassion and never inflict harm on others, even in the name of "justice." Our suffering is due to our own destructive actions done in this or previous lives.

Reading sutras, performing chanted meditations, and making offerings in times of distress are done for two reasons. First, these actions purify the imprints of our destructive actions so they won't ripen in the future. In addition, they create positive potential, which will bring happiness as its result. Sometimes these ceremonies are held in the homes of the devotees, while at other times they are held in the temple or monastery.

When people die, the Sangha is often requested to do chanted meditations for the benefit of the deceased. Some of the chanted texts may be instructions to the dying or dead person, to help him or her have a good rebirth. Others accumulate positive potential, which is then dedicated to all beings, but especially for the benefit of the dying or dead.

Although in Asian cultures, monastics are usually asked to conduct these ceremonies, lay followers may also do them. In Western Dharma centers, lay followers and Sangha generally perform them together. People shouldn't have the attitude, "I'm a lay person so I can't do chanted meditations." Nor should they think they're hiring the Sangha to do it for them, while they relax. When we have close connections with others, it's extremely beneficial if we pray, read Dharma texts, make offerings, and do chanted meditations for their benefit.

Buddhist festivals are many and varied. What has been explained here is only a limited sample. Feel free to visit Buddhist temples, monasteries, or Dharma centers on festival days. Ask practitioners about the significance of the ceremonies and holidays. Also, when you visit temples, you needn't engage in practices you don't understand—bowing, for example. The spirit of Buddhism is one of free inquiry and understanding. Let's take advantage of this openness to learn.

V   BUDDHISM TODAY

Buddhism in the twenty-first century faces two challenges. The first is to clarify people's misconceptions about it. For example, some people confuse Buddhism with ancestor worship, others with fortune-telling. These issues need to be clarified for us to properly understand the Buddha's teachings.

In addition, religious harmony is essential for world peace. Buddhism is renowned for its tolerance and appreciation of other religions, yet Buddhists remain firm on their own path. How does this remarkable attitude come about?

1 WHAT IS BUDDHISM, WHAT IS SUPERSTITION?: WHAT BUDDHISM SAYS ABOUT GHOSTS, FORTUNE-TELLING, AND PSYCHIC POWERS

The Buddha's teachings deal with mental development. The actual path to enlightenment is the realization of emptiness in a person's mind. This path can't be altered according to time and place. However, the external forms that Buddhism takes vary from country to country as rites and rituals are integrated with the cultural forms of each place.

Sometimes the integration of Buddhism with native cultures has led to a lack of clear distinction between Buddhist and non-Buddhist practices. Although the Sangha know the difference between native traditions and Buddhist practices and maintain a high standard in Buddhist practice, in the lives of many lay people, these are mixed.

For example, some people consider themselves Buddhists and have a statue of the Buddha flanked by Chinese gods in their temple. They are unclear about the difference between the Buddhas and bodhisattvas and the native worldly gods, and thus pray to all of them equally. Some of the practices performed in these temples—going into trance, fortune-telling, and so on—are not Buddhist practices. They are folk customs, popularized Taoism, or ancestor worship.

Helping Deceased Relatives

One example of people thinking a practice of ancestor worship is Buddhism is the burning of paper goods and money for deceased relatives. Folk culture believes that after death, everyone is reborn in a spirit netherworld similar to our human world with houses, clothes, credit cards, and so forth. Living family members wish to demonstrate filial piety and provide for their deceased relatives. They also want to prevent neglected spirits from harming them. To do this, they burn paper houses, clothes, etc. to offer them to their deceased relatives. They believe this transfers the goods to the netherworld where their deceased relatives enjoy them.

Burning paper goods is ancestor worship, not Buddhism. According to Buddhism, people aren't born in a spirit netherworld after death. Instead, they enter an intermediate state (*bardo*) before being reborn in another body. The intermediate state may be as short as one moment or as long as forty-nine days, after which they are definitely reborn. Intermediate state beings do not have the ability to communicate with us nor we with them. Only other intermediate state beings and people with clairvoyance attained through meditation can perceive intermediate state beings.

After the intermediate state, people are reborn in one of the six realms of cyclic existence—god, demi-god, human, animal, hungry ghost, and hellish being. While some beings are reborn as spirits, who are included in the hungry ghost realm, not everyone is. Rebirth in any realm is temporary, not eternal, and people's previous actions or karma influence into which realm they are reborn.

Our deceased relatives will have possessions according to the realm in which they are born. For example, if Grandma died one year ago, by now she has been reborn in another realm. If she was reborn as a human, she is now a tiny baby. She (or maybe he because we may change gender from one lifetime to the next) has food and shelter provided by her new parents. Burning paper dresses doesn't give Grandma new baby clothes.

Although it's natural to miss our loved ones when they die, trying to contact them through mediums isn't beneficial. The Buddha's first teaching was about the transience of life. Our minds will be more peaceful if we accept the death of our loved ones.

It's good to want to help departed relatives and friends, and there are Buddhist practices to do this. We can offer the deceased's possessions to charities or to religious institutions and practitioners. Also, we can do special prayers and practices or request the Sangha to do them, and dedicate the positive potential of these actions for those who are deceased.

We cannot transfer our good karma to others like transferring money from one bank account to another, for the person who does the action is the one who experiences the karmic result. However, by dedicating our positive potential for the well-being of deceased ones, we create conducive circumstances whereby their previously created good karma can ripen. The good karmic imprints on their mindstreams are like seeds in a field. Our prayers and dedication of positive potential resemble the water and fertilizer that make the seeds grow.

The best way to help our parents have a good rebirth is to encourage them to act positively and stop acting destructively while they're alive. Thus, let's encourage our family to be generous and patient with others. Let's not ask them to lie on our behalf or to deceive others to get more money for the family. In this way, they'll have many good karmic imprints and few bad ones to carry with them to future lives.

The Festival of the Seventh Month and Ullambana

The Festival of the Seventh Month is particularly confusing for many Asians. This is a non-Buddhist holiday of ancestor worship celebrated in Taiwan, Singapore, Malaysia, and other countries. It is often confused with the Buddhist holiday of Ullambana, celebrated on the fifteenth day of the same month. The mix-up between the two arose because both festivals occur during the seventh lunar month, and both are done to benefit deceased relatives. However, the philosophy and practice of the two are quite different.

In ancestor worship one sets out food and incense offerings to ancestral tablets or to effigies of deceased relatives in the seventh lunar month. Also, paper money, houses, and so forth are burned in the hope that the dead will receive and enjoy them. According to folk belief, the beings in the hellish realm are released for a month and roam the earth. To provide for their needs and to win their favor and prevent them from harming the living, relatives make offerings to them.

However, as explained above, not everyone is reborn as a spirit, and burned goods don't reach them. Also, spirits belong to the hungry ghost realm and don't live in the hellish realm. In addition, according to Buddhism, those who are temporarily born in unfortunate states such as the hellish realms don't have a holiday in the seventh month during which they roam around our world.

The Buddhist festival of Ullambana falls on the fifteenth day of the seventh month. It stems from the *Ullambana Sutra*, found in the Chinese Buddhist Canon. This sutra tells the story of Maudgalyayana, one of the Buddha's foremost disciples, who by means of clairvoyance saw that his mother had been reborn as a hungry ghost. He lovingly brought her some food, which she hid because she was too miserly to share it with others. When she later took it out, it was rotten. Saddened, Maudgalyayana wanted to help his mother's plight but didn't know how.

He asked advice from the Buddha, who recommended he make offerings of food and other necessities to the assembly of Sangha, request them to meditate, and dedicate the positive potentials created by both himself and the Sangha for his mother's benefit. Maudgalyayana did this on the fifteenth day of the seventh month. The resultant positive potential helped his mother's own previously created positive potential (good karma) to ripen. Her life as a hungry ghost ended, and she was reborn in more fortunate circumstances.

Thus, many Chinese and Japanese Buddhists celebrate Ullambana by offering to the Sangha, requesting them to do prayers and meditation, and dedicating the positive potential for the benefit of departed relatives and friends. Thus, we can see Ullambana is different in content and philosophy from the non-Buddhist Festival of the Seventh Month.

Spirits and Gods

According to Buddhism, some people may be temporarily reborn as spirits due to the actions they did in the past. Among the six realms, spirits are generally considered to be in the hungry ghost realm, although some may be in the god (*deva*) realm. . Both spirits and gods can speak through mediums.

Generally, when a medium goes into trance, his or her consciousness is temporarily suppressed, and a spirit or god speaks through the medium's body. Spirits may be helpful or harmful, just as human beings may help or harm us. Spirits and gods are worldly beings, subject to birth and death in cyclic existence. They lack the perfect wisdom and compassion of the Buddhas. Some spirits and gods have limited clairvoyant powers. Thus, sometimes their predictions are accurate, while other times they are not. They may identify themselves as a deceased relative or as a bodhisattva, but that doesn't mean they actually are.

Consulting spirits and gods that speak through mediums is cultural.

The Buddha did not teach this as a Dharma practice. He taught the path to enlightenment and encouraged us to develop our own wisdom to make decisions. It's our responsibility to reflect whether the action we're going to do is ethical or not. Is it motivated by genuine loving-kindness or by anger, attachment, or confusion?

In some cultures, people fear being harmed by spirits. Spirits can harm humans only when a person has created the cause to be harmed—that is, if he or she has harmed others in this or previous lives. There is no benefit in fearing spirits. In fact, fear and paranoia open the door to receive spirit harm. Even if a real spirit doesn't harm, a fearful person's mind can create an imaginary spirit that does.

Dreaming about the deceased doesn't indicate that they have returned. This is most likely a product of our imagination. When we dream of an apple, it isn't a real apple. Likewise, when we dream about a dead relative, it isn't that person.

When people are afraid of spirits or are being harmed by them, refuge and compassion are the best antidotes. If we imagine the Buddha and take strong refuge in the Buddha, Dharma, and Sangha, spirits can't harm us, and the fear soon disappears.

Spirits are sentient beings just as are human beings. They want to be happy and not have suffering, just as we do. Understanding this, we can feel compassion for them and wish them to be free from all misery. Loving-kindness and compassion prevent us from being fearful because we're more concerned with others—in this case the spirit—than with ourselves. Just as most people don't intentionally harm someone who has compassion for them, spirits won't harm someone who wishes them well.

Some Buddhists may make offerings to certain spirits as a way to bring them happiness or prevent them from harming. They may ask worldly protectors for help with affairs of this life. However, in doing so, it is important not to take ultimate refuge in these beings. They are limited beings like us, trapped in cyclic existence. While at times they may help, they are unable to lead us to enlightenment. Propitiating them while ignoring our Buddhist practice is not proper.

In conclusion, it's wiser for us to practice the Buddha's teachings as explained in the four noble truths and the gradual path to enlightenment than to get involved with worldly spirits. Like other sentient beings, spirits can be objects of our compassion.

Geomancy and Fortune-telling

Geomancy, the positioning of buildings, furniture, graves, and so forth to bring good fortune and prosperity, is an art developed in East Asian cultures. It isn't part of Buddhism, although some Chinese Buddhists practice it. Buddhists may play chess, but that doesn't mean chess is Buddhism. Geomancy is similar: it comes from the general culture of a country.

Some Buddhists—and non-Buddhists, too—consult fortune-tellers. However, that doesn't mean fortune-telling is a Buddhist practice. Although some people like to consult fortune-tellers, psychics, astrologers, or tarot-card readers, it's unwise to overemphasize their predictions. To paraphrase His Holiness the Dalai Lama, "We never know the future until it happens."

Asking Buddhist monastics to give a lottery-winning number is inappropriate. Spinning wheels in front of a Buddha statue to get a lucky number is similarly incorrect, especially since the Buddha discouraged people from wasting their money on gambling.

Clairvoyance

Some people are fascinated by supernatural powers and seek them as the goal of spiritual practice. However, the aim of practicing Dharma isn't to attain clairvoyance; it's to receive enlightenment for the benefit of others.

Ordinary clairvoyance can come from a variety of causes. It may be due to karma—previous lives' actions and prayers. This clairvoyance isn't always reliable and is lost at death.

True and reliable clairvoyance is attained through meditative concentration. Here, clairvoyance comes as a by-product of meditation, just as when one buys rice, the bag comes along with it. One needn't cultivate clairvoyance separately.

A person's motivation determines whether or not their psychic powers are beneficial. Those who seek reputation and material offerings as a result of having psychic powers have worldly motivations. Those who are proud and boast about their clairvoyance risk using it to enhance their egos rather than subdue them. They may misuse their powers, causing suffering for themselves and others. For these reasons, an impartial loving and compassionate attitude toward all beings is essential in order to use psychic powers wisely.

The Buddha forbade his disciples to brag about their attainments or to use their supernatural abilities flamboyantly. True spiritual practitioners are humble. They prefer to quietly serve others rather than to draw attention and admiration to themselves.

Having clairvoyance isn't special. All of us have had it in previous lives. But it hasn't done us much good, for we're still taking rebirth in cyclic existence due to the force of our afflictions and karma.

Practicing the path to enlightenment, however, brings lasting benefit for others and ourselves. Therefore, let's use the great opportunity we have in this lifetime to study and practice the Dharma. The best "magical power" is a kind heart and a sense of universal responsibility caring for the welfare of all beings. These qualities are more rare and valuable than clairvoyant powers.

If we are sincerely interested in attaining enlightenment for the benefit of all beings, then it's essential to be able to discriminate the path described by the Buddha from cultural customs, superstition, and misguided paths. To do this, we listen to teachings from qualified masters and then examine them carefully and ask questions to clarify our doubts. By practicing the correct path, we'll be able to attain enlightenment.

2 RELIGIOUS HARMONY:
DIVERSITY IS BENEFICIAL

The teachings I heard at my first meditation course deeply changed my life. What impressed me wasn't that they were Buddhist teachings but that they made sense. I didn't care who spoke them or what the name of the religion was because my real interest was in the meaning of the teachings and their significance in my daily life.

At that time, I didn't know the terms Mahayana and Theravada, nor did I care. I didn't understand the words Nyingma, Kagyu, Gelug, and Sakya. Zen, Pure Land, Vajrayana were just names to me. To this day, I feel uncomfortable when people ask which Buddhist tradition I follow, for in my heart I'm simply another human being seeking the path to happiness and a way to make my life meaningful to others.

Labels too often divide people. Instead of understanding the real meaning and purpose of something, we're attached to the name. We judge others on the basis of the labels attached to them, rather than trying to understand who they really are or what they believe. We create a general conception of what a certain name means, and then we assume that everyone who has that label is alike. Our limited minds think, "If you're a Theravadin, you don't listen to Mahayana teachings. If you're a Christian, you're not a Buddhist. If you're religious, you're not scientific."

On the basis of thinking, "I'm a 'this' and they're a 'that,'" we argue. This happens amongst Buddhists and between Buddhists and those of other religions. Fortunately, no wars have ever been fought in the name of the Buddha or in order to protect or spread Buddhism. Nevertheless, any kind of closed-minded sectarian attitude is harmful, for it not only impedes our own spiritual progress, it also causes friction among people.

How does sectarianism harm our own progress? In Buddhism, the two chief qualities we want to develop are wisdom and compassion. If we're attached to our own religion, we take it as a personal affront when someone disagrees with what we believe. Becoming angry and aggressive, we defend our beliefs and attack those of others. At this point, we stop seeking the truth and start defending our religion simply because it's ours.

Such angry confusion leaves negative karmic imprints on our mindstreams. Obscuring our minds, these imprints prevent us from gaining wisdom. In addition, anger is totally opposite to compassion, the wish for all others to be free from suffering. Thus, sectarianism hinders our development of wisdom and compassion and leads us further from enlightenment rather than toward it.

Harmony among Buddhist Traditions

Having a general overview of the path to enlightenment enables us to understand that all teachings given by the Buddha are advice he gave to students about how to practice at different stages of their development. None of the teachings are to be abandoned, neglected, or criticized for they all are suitable to practice at some level of our development. If we criticize the Buddha's teachings and thus neglect to test and practice them, we're abandoning the very methods that can lead us to realizations.

This doesn't mean, however, that we need to practice all the teachings at this very moment. What the Buddha taught is vast and profound, and we have to approach it gradually. We practice whatever corresponds to our dispositions and whatever we're capable of at the present. There is no pressure to do everything immediately. Slowly, we'll evolve and can integrate more teachings into our practice. Temporarily leaving aside some of the teachings because they're beyond our scope is different from criticizing them.

People have the tendency to want to be the best. But what does "the best" mean? Children's books are best for children and adult books are best for adults. We can't say that either children's or adults' books are *the* best. Similarly, it's best for someone to read English books if that's the only language he or she knows, but for a Chinese-speaking person, Chinese literature is best. There is no absolute "best" that applies to everyone.

The essential point is to realize that not everyone is alike. We may like one food and someone else may like another, but both foods nourish and sustain life. Likewise, one person may be attracted to the Theravadin tradition and another to the Mahayana, but both traditions enable people to improve themselves and to progress on the path. This applies also to people who follow Buddhism and those who don't. As long as a philosophy encourages people to avoid harming others and to help them as much as possible, it's beneficial.

It's not wise to criticize other Buddhist traditions because their ways of practice are different from ours. For example, some people are inspired by devotion, ritual, and prayer. Other people don't find these appealing and prefer silent meditation. We aren't all alike, nor should we be. It's wonderful that so many Buddhist traditions exist, so each of us can find one that suits our personality and helps us to develop.

Similarly, we shouldn't criticize any of the Buddha's teachings if we feel they don't fit us. The Buddha gave teachings that corresponded to the mentality of his audience. For example, the Buddha taught different views of selflessness according to the audience to which he was speaking. From this, four main philosophical schools arose, each based on different sutras and each with its own assertion of the meaning of selflessness.

It's unwise for us to disdain any of these views or schools, for they are suitable for certain groups of people, at particular levels of development. Let's not be proud and think, "I study the highest view. There's no need for me to learn the others." In fact, the great masters say we can't understand the final view of selflessness unless we have previously understood those of the other schools.

The diversity of philosophical assertions is stimulating. It makes us wonder, "Which is the final view? How do things really exist?" To answer this, we have to learn and examine all views. In this way our wisdom increases. Realizing emptiness isn't a matter of repeating by rote a certain dogma. It depends on understanding, and this comes through thinking about the various philosophical views.

Let's avoid criticizing other traditions because they use terms differently than we do. One word may have different meanings in various traditions. If we forget this fact, we may read a book from another tradition and impose our definitions onto certain words, distorting their meaning in that context. Then, of course, those teachings won't make sense to us. However, if we have vast learning, then we'll understand the various meanings of the terms correctly and will see that the various traditions come to the same point.

Referring to the difference in vocabulary used by the four Tibetan Buddhist traditions to describe the final stage of the practice, His Holiness the Dalai Lama said in *Kindness, Clarity, and Insight,* "Transcending sectarianism, we can find much to evoke deep realization by seeing how these schools come down to the same basic thought."

Both the bodhisattva vows and the tantric vows contain injunctions against disparaging any of the Buddha's teachings. The *Sutra of an All-Inclusive Interweaving of Everything* states:

> O Manjushri, to regard some of the enlightening words spoken by the Tathagata (Buddha) as good and some as bad is to discard the Dharma. To say this is reasonable while that is not...(or) this was spoken (only) for the sake of bodhisattvas and that was spoken (only) for hearers...(or) this is something in which bodhisattvas need not train is to discard the Dharma.

Buddhism and Other Religions

The great leaders of all the world's religions have sought to benefit others by sharing with them their own spiritual experiences. However, common people have become attached to the names of those experiences and philosophies and have fought with those who didn't agree or whose faith had a different name. The number of people who have been killed in the name of religion throughout history is appalling. None of the founders of the world's great religions would be pleased by the amount of blood that has been shed in their names.

The great holy beings aren't attached to labels because they seek meaning, harmony, and love. They have no need to prove that they are right and that theirs is the only way. Most of the great religious leaders have lived simply and have found happiness within themselves. They haven't sought praise, wealth, power, or glory. Hostile sectarianism and religious prejudice aren't the way of the holy people of any religion, for they want their followers to live in peace with all other beings.

All religions share certain crucial points. They recognize that material development alone isn't the path to happiness and that a greater happiness than that received through our senses exists. All religions strive to help humans improve themselves by developing patience, love, and respect for each other. They want people to cultivate good attitudes toward one another and then to implement these in service to the larger community. To this end, all faiths propound ethical values to help us regulate our behavior. In *Kindness, Clarity, and Insight*, His Holiness the Dalai Lama says:

> The motivation of all religious practice is similar—love, sincerity, honesty. The way of life of practically all religious persons is contentment. The teachings of tolerance, love, and compassion are the same. A basic goal is the benefit of humankind—each type of system seeking in its own unique ways to improve human beings. If we put too much emphasis on our philosophy, religion, or theory, are too attached to it, and try to impose it on other people, it makes trouble. Basically all the great teachers, such as Gautama Buddha, Jesus Christ, or Mohammed, founded their new teachings with a motivation of helping their fellow humans. They did not mean to gain anything for themselves or to create more trouble or unrest in the world.

Being a Buddhist doesn't mean bowing to the Buddha, chanting Buddhist prayers, or having a shrine with a statue of the Buddha. The essence of Buddhism is wisdom and compassion, and these can be expressed and shared with others without any Buddhist terminology. Similarly, the essence of Christian, Hindu, Jewish, and Islamic teachings is ethical discipline and love. These qualities are universal.

In terms of philosophy, there are differences—some religions believe in a creator God, while others, like Buddhism, do not. It is naive to say that all religious philosophies are the same. Perhaps from the viewpoint of those who have realized and experienced them, they are. It could be that the mystical experiences of holy beings of all religions are the same, but the expressions of these in words and concepts are different. Words are limiting; they are facsimiles of reality. Thus, the experience may be the same, but the words describing it may differ.

However, for us ordinary beings, concepts point out the direction to the experience. Therefore, we must analyze the various philosophies and determine which one best enables us to purify our minds and develop our good qualities. There is no need to criticize others because different philosophies appeal to them. Although we may discuss and debate philosophy together, pointing out inconsistencies in one and virtues of another, this doesn't mean we put down the people who believe them.

From a Buddhist point of view, the diversity of philosophies is beneficial, for not everyone sees things in the same way. We're all at different levels; we have different interests and inclinations. Therefore, it's beneficial for a wide range of religions to exist so everyone can find something suitable for his or her character. It would be terrible if we all had to fit into one mold and think in exactly the same way. Also, that would be impossible. His Holiness the Dalai Lama said,

> I think that differences in faith are useful. There is richness in the
> fact that there are so many different presentations of the way. Given
> that there are so many different types of people with various pre-
> dispositions and inclinations, this is helpful.

Interfaith Dialogue

In Europe, North America, and Australia, interfaith dialogue is increasing. When the Dalai Lama goes to Europe, he is hosted by the Vatican. One high official in the Episcopalian Church introduced His Holiness when he spoke at Westminster Abbey in 1985. Some Tibetan monastics have visited Catholic monasteries in America, and some American Catholic monastics have stayed in Japanese Buddhist temples. Within Buddhism, there are international conferences and seminars attended by representatives of all Buddhist traditions. These are just a few instances; there are many more.

Although it's essential for world peace that today's great religious leaders meet and learn from each other, it's equally important for common practitioners to do so as well. Not only does interfaith dialogue enable us to pray and meditate together and thus share our internal peace, it also helps to prevent superstition, misconceptions, and fear of other religious groups.

Personally, I've benefited greatly from discussions with people of other faiths. I understand better how the human mind works and how to communicate with people in ways that they understand. My mind becomes more flexible and can look beyond the words people use to the meanings they express. I've also received some excellent guidance as well: When a Catholic nun who had been ordained over fifty years told me of the various stages of development she experienced on her religious journey and the obstacles she had to overcome, I saw many parallels with Buddhist practice. This gave me, a younger nun, courage to go through the difficult times in the practice.

Once I spoke with a female Baptist minister, and we compared our experiences as women in religion. This was very rewarding and stimulating. Speaking with a Jewish rabbi, I was astonished to learn that some ancient Jewish worship practices resembled Buddhist ones. When reading a book on Christian contemplation, I noticed it was similar to the "guru yoga" practice in Tibetan Buddhism. These experiences have helped me to appreciate both the diversity and the unity in human religious thought.

Appreciating others' religions and beliefs doesn't jeopardize our commitment to our own. Rather, as we look beyond the words to their meaning, as we look beyond superficial differences to a common aim, our wisdom and compassion will grow, and our own faith in the Three Jewels will increase.

GLOSSARY

AFFLICTIONS   Disturbing attitudes and negative emotions such as ignorance, attachment, anger, pride, jealousy, and confusion that disturb
our mental peace and propel us to act in ways harmful to others.

AFFLICTIVE OBSCURATIONS   Afflictions and karma that cause rebirth in cyclic existence. When the afflictive obscurations are removed, one becomes an arhat.

ALTRUISTIC INTENTION (BODHICHITTA)   The mind dedicated to attaining
enlightenment in order to benefit all sentient beings.

ARHAT   A person who has attained liberation and is thus free from cyclic
existence.

BHIKSHU (BHIKKHU), BHIKSHUNI (BHIKKHUNI)   A fully-ordained monk or
nun, respectively.

BODHISATTVA   A person who has developed the spontaneous altruistic intention.

BUDDHA   Any person who has purified all defilements and developed all
good qualities. "The Buddha" refers to Shakyamuni Buddha, who lived
2,500 years ago in India.

BUDDHA FIGURE   A manifestation of the Buddha; a Buddhist deity.

BUDDHA-NATURE (BUDDHA-POTENTIAL)   The innate qualities of the mind
enabling all beings to attain enlightenment.

CESSATION   The extinguishment of an obscuration—for example, anger—

so that it can never arise again. When all afflictions have been eliminated, we attain nirvana.

COMPASSION   The wish for sentient beings to be free from suffering and its causes.

COGNITIVE OBSCURATIONS   Stains of the afflictions that prevent perceiving all existent phenomena. When both afflictive obscurations and cognitive obscurations have been removed, we become a fully enlightened Buddha.

CYCLIC EXISTENCE   Uncontrollably being reborn under the influence of afflictions and karmic imprints.

DEPENDENT ARISING   The fact that all phenomena are dependent on the parts of which they are made and on the mind that conceives and labels them. Many phenomena—our body, tables, and so forth—also depend on causes and conditions to exist.

DETERMINATION TO BE FREE   The attitude aspiring to be free from all problems and sufferings and to attain liberation.

DHARMA   Our wisdom realizing emptiness and the absence of suffering and its causes that this wisdom brings. In a more general sense, Dharma refers to the teachings and doctrine of the Buddha.

EMPOWERMENT   A ceremony in Vajrayana Buddhism in which the disciple is authorized to meditate on a particular manifestation of the Buddha. Also called "initiation."

EMPTINESS   The lack of independent or inherent existence. This is the ultimate nature or reality of all persons and phenomena.

ENLIGHTENMENT (BUDDHAHOOD)   The state of a Buddha, i.e., the state of having forever eliminated all obscurations from our mindstream and having developed our good qualities and wisdom to their fullest extent. Buddhahood supersedes liberation.

HEARERS   Followers of the Buddha who aspire to become arhats. They are so called because they hear the Buddha's doctrine and then teach it to others.

IMPRINT   The residual energy left on the mindstream when an action has been completed. When it matures, it influences our experience.

IMPUTE   To give a label or name to an object; to give meaning to an object.

INHERENT OR INDEPENDENT EXISTENCE   A false and non-existent quality that we project onto persons and phenomena; existence independent of causes and conditions, parts, or the mind labeling a phenomenon.

INITIATION   *See* Empowerment.

KARMA   Intentional action. Our actions leave imprints on our mindstreams, which bring about our experiences.

LIBERATION   Freedom from cyclic existence.

LOVE   The wish for sentient beings to have happiness and its causes.

MAHAYANA   The Buddhist tradition that asserts that all beings can attain enlightenment. It strongly emphasizes the development of compassion and the altruistic intention.

MANTRA   A series of syllables consecrated by a Buddha and expressing the essence of the entire path to enlightenment. They are recited to concentrate and purify the mind.

MEDITATION   Habituating ourselves with positive attitudes and correct perspectives.

MEDITATIVE QUIESCENCE   The ability to remain single-pointedly on the object of meditation with a pliant and blissful mind. It is also called calm abiding.

MIND   The experiential, cognitive part of living beings. Non-physical, the mind isn't made of atoms, nor is it perceivable through our five senses.

MINDSTREAM   The continuity of the mind.

MONASTICS   Monks and nuns.

NIRVANA   The cessation of suffering and its causes.

POSITIVE POTENTIAL   Imprints of positive actions, which will result in happiness in the future. Sometimes translated as "merit" or "good karma."

PURE LAND   A Mahayana Buddhist tradition emphasizing methods to be reborn in a pure land. A pure land is a place established by a Buddha or bodhisattva where all conditions are conducive for the practice of Dharma and the attainment of enlightenment.

REALIZATION   A clear, deep, and correct understanding of what the Buddha taught. This may be either conceptual or non-conceptual direct experience. The non-conceptual direct realizations gained at higher levels of the path cleanse the obscurations from our minds forever.

SAMSARA   Cyclic existence.

SANGHA   Any person who directly and non-conceptually realizes emptiness. In a more general sense, Sangha refers to the communities of ordained monks and nuns. It is sometimes used to refer to Buddhists in general.

SELFLESSNESS   The absence of a fantasized way of existence.

SOLITARY REALIZERS   Followers of the Buddha who aspire for arhatship and who attain nirvana during times when a Buddha hasn't appeared in the world.

SPECIAL INSIGHT (*vipassana, vipashyana*)   A wisdom thoroughly discriminating phenomena. When conjoined with meditative quiescence, it enables us to analyze the meditation object and simultaneously remain single-pointedly on it. This removes ignorance.

SUFFERING (*dukkha*)   Any unsatisfactory condition. It doesn't refer only to physical or mental pain, but includes all problematic and unsatisfactory conditions.

SUTRA   A scripture containing a teaching of the Buddha. Sutras are found in all Buddhist traditions.

TAKING REFUGE   Entrusting our spiritual development to the guidance of the Buddha, Dharma, and Sangha.

TANTRA   A scripture describing the Vajrayana practice. This term can also refer to the Vajrayana practice.

THERAVADA   The tradition of the elders. A Buddhist tradition popular in Southeast Asia and Sri Lanka.

THREE JEWELS   Also called the Triple Gem, refers to the Buddha, Dharma, and Sangha.

VAJRAYANA   A Mahayana Buddhist tradition popular in Tibet and Japan.

WISDOM REALIZING REALITY (WISDOM REALIZING EMPTINESS)   A view that correctly understands the manner in which all persons and phenomena exist, i.e., the mind realizing the emptiness of inherent existence.

WORLDLY DEITIES AND WORLDLY SPIRITS   Beings born in the god realm or as powerful spirits. As they still take rebirth in cyclic existence under the force of afflictions and karma, their powers are limited and temporary.

ZEN (CH'AN)   A Mahayana Buddhist tradition popular in China and Japan.

ADDITIONAL READING

Berzin, Alexander. *Relating to a Spiritual Teacher: Building a Healthy Relationship.* Ithaca, N.Y.: Snow Lion Publications, 2000.

Buddhadasa Bhikkhu. *Heartwood of the Bodhi Tree: The Buddha's Teaching on Voidness.* Boston: Wisdom Publications, 1994.

Buddhadasa Bhikkhu. *Mindfulness with Breathing.* Boston: Wisdom Publications, 1996.

Chodron, Thubten. *Blossoms of the Dharma: Living as a Buddhist Nun.* Berkeley: North Atlantic Books, 2000.

Chodron, Thubten. *Buddhism for Beginners.* Ithaca, N.Y.: Snow Lion Publications, 2001.

Chodron, Thubten. *Open Heart, Clear Mind.* Ithaca, N.Y.: Snow Lion Publications, 1990.

Chodron, Thubten. *Working with Anger.* Ithaca, N.Y.: Snow Lion Publications, 2001.

Dhammananda, K. Sri. *How to Live without Fear and Worry.* Kuala Lumpur: Buddhist Missionary Society, 1989.

Dhammananda, K. Sri. *What Buddhists Believe.* Kuala Lumpur: Buddhist Missionary Society, 1987.

Dhammananda, K. Sri, ed. *The Dhammapada.* Kuala Lumpur: Sasana Abhiwurdhi Wardhana Society, 1988.

Dharmarakshita. *The Wheel of Sharp Weapons.* Dharamsala, India: Library of Tibetan Works and Archives, 1981.

Dilgo Khyentse Rinpoche. *Enlightened Courage*. Ithaca, N.Y.: Snow Lion Publications, 1993.

Eppsteiner, Fred, ed. *The Path of Compassion*. Berkeley: Parallax Press, 1988.

Gampopa. *The Jewel Ornament of Liberation*. Trans. Khenpo Konchog Gyaltsen Rinpoche. Ithaca, N.Y.: Snow Lion Publications, 1998.

Goldstein, Joseph. *The Experience of Insight*. Boston: Shambhala, 1987.

H. H. Tenzin Gyatso, the Fourteenth Dalai Lama. *Kindness, Clarity, and Insight*. Ithaca, N.Y.: Snow Lion Publications, 1984.

H. H. Tenzin Gyatso, the Fourteenth Dalai Lama. *The Dalai Lama at Harvard*. Ithaca, N.Y.: Snow Lion Publications, 1989.

Jampa Tegchok, Geshe. *Transforming the Heart: The Buddhist Way to Joy and Courage*. Ithaca, N.Y.: Snow Lion Publications, 1999.

Kapleau, Philip, ed. *The Three Pillars of Zen*. London: Rider, 1980.

Khema, Ayya. *Being Nobody, Going Nowhere*. Boston: Wisdom Publications, 1987.

McDonald, Kathleen. *How to Meditate*. Boston: Wisdom Publications, 1984.

Nhat Hanh, Thich. *Being Peace*. Berkeley: Parallax Press, 1987.

Nyanaponika, Thera. *The Heart of Buddhist Meditation*. London: Rider, 1962.

Rabten, Geshe, and Geshe Dhargyey. *Advice from a Spiritual Friend*. Boston: Wisdom Publications, 1986.

Schumann, H. W. *The Historical Buddha*. London: Arkana, 1989.

Sonam Rinchen, Geshe. *The Thirty-seven Practices of Bodhisattvas*. Translated and edited by Ruth Sonam. Ithaca, N.Y.: Snow Lion Publications, 1996.

Sparham, Gareth, trans. *The Tibetan Dhammapada*. Boston: Wisdom Publications, 1983.

Stevenson, Ian. *Cases of the Reincarnation Type*. 4 vols. Charlottesville: University of Virginia Press, 1975.

Story, Francis. *Rebirth as Doctrine and Experience.* Kandy: Buddhist Publication Society, 1975.

Suzuki, D. T. *An Introduction to Zen Buddhism.* London: Rider, 1969.

Suzuki, Shunryu. *Zen Mind, Beginner's Mind.* New York: Weatherhill, 1980.

Thubten Yeshe, Lama. *Introduction to Tantra.* Boston: Wisdom Publications, 1987.

Thubten Zopa Rinpoche. *The Door to Satisfaction.* Boston: Wisdom Publications, 1994.

Thubten Zopa Rinpoche. *Transforming Problems into Happiness.* Boston: Wisdom Publications, 2001.

Trungpa, Chogyam. *Cutting Through Spiritual Materialism.* Berkeley: Shambhala, 1973.

Tsomo, Karma Lekshe, ed. *Daughters of the Buddha.* Ithaca, N.Y.: Snow Lion Publications, 1988.

Tsongkhapa, Je. *The Three Principal Aspects of the Path.* Howell, N.J.: Mahayana Sutra and Tantra Press, 1988.

Wangchen, Geshe. *Awakening the Mind of Enlightenment.* Boston: Wisdom Publications, 1988.

Warder, A. K. *Indian Buddhism.* Delhi: Motilal Banarsidass, 1980.

Willis, Janice D., ed. *Feminine Ground.* Ithaca, N.Y.: Snow Lion Publications, 1987.

Wu Yin, Bhikshuni. *Choosing Simplicity: A Commentary on the Bhikshuni Pratimoksha.* Ithaca, N.Y.: Snow Lion Publications, 2001.